GATHERING

OTHER TITLES BY BASIL DU TOIT

Home Truths, Carrefour Press
Older Women, Snailpress
From the City of Ideas, Touchpaper Press
Old, Smith | Doorstop

Gathering Photons

in May

Dear Miranda
I hope you find aspects of
this book interesting; with
affection and admiration
from Bas

Collected Sonnets

Volume One

Basil du Toit

Published by New Generation Publishing in 2023

Copyright © Basil du Toit 2023

First Edition

The author asserts the moral right under the Copyright, Designs and Patents Act 1988 to be identified as the author of this work.

All Rights reserved. No part of this publication may be reproduced, stored in a retrieval system or transmitted, in any form or by any means without the prior consent of the author, nor be otherwise circulated in any form of binding or cover other than that in which it is published and without a similar condition being imposed on the subsequent purchaser.

ISBN: 978-1-80369-758-1

www.newgeneration-publishing.com

New Generation Publishing

die glasharten
Schleifgeräuche der Schrift

the glasshard
grinding sounds of writing

Paul Celan, *Fadensonnen*

Gathering Photons in May, Volume One of Collected Sonnets

UNIFORM WITH THIS VOLUME:

Playing With My Christianity, Volume Two of Collected Sonnets
In a Mexican Dialect of Fortran, Volume Three of Collected Sonnets

ACKNOWLEDGEMENTS:

Versions of some of these poems have appeared in the following publications:

Anima, Antiphon, Carapace, Dawntreader, Envoi, Interpreter's House, Lighthouse, Orbis, Poetry Salzburg Review, Raum, Southlight, Stanzas

The artwork on which the cover is based is a study of Coney Island by Eve Ferguson. My sincerest thanks to her for permission to use her work.

This volume is dedicated to Sheena Williamson, the first reader of these poems – in gratitude for her inspired and generous responses.

Edinburgh, Scotland
2023

Contents

According to Plato	1
Elegy on the Decommissioning of Dounreay	2
Paean to Human Flesh	3
The Dogs of Love	4
Philosophy at War	5
Psychology Under the Covers	6
Viewed From Below	7
Inclinations of Nature	8
The Hardness of Psychological Material	9
New Light in Old Mornings	10
Deltas	11
Borderlights	12
The Laws of the Other	13
A Punishment Stick	14
Boarded Up for the Season	15
Smitten Oak	16
Unspeakable	17
An Attempt at Diagnosis	18
Thinking Back to Then	19
Transaction	20
Empathising With a Circular Saw	21
Stringed Woodnotes	22
The Sun King's Eclipse	23
Turning the Baby Around	24
Maintenance Stopover	25
House Anthropology	26
Campus Muse	27
Restricted Access	28

String Theory in the Poetry of Donne	29
Croc Engineering in the Okavango	30
Smoke and Honey	31
English in the Cretaceous	32
Hydrogen & Co	33
Atheism in Action – The Fine Print	34
Impudence of the Hand	35
Looking Rosier by the Minute	36
From the School of Atheism	37
An Ecumenical Matter	38
Speaking Up for Northern Light	39
Cancelling My Religion	40
Fanfare for a New Season	41
Sun Breathing	42
Surgical Words	43
A Sipping Acquaintance	44
Stowaway	45
The Blakean Body Shop	46
Maori Shell Music	47
Kant Reaches for an Orange	48
Pumpkin Music	49
Through World-Tinted Spectacles	50
Trojan Gifts	51
Old Sopranos Singing Bach	52
Atheism in Action – The Choir	53
Song of Songs	54
Leaves & Locusts	55
Our Life Together	56
A Spurning of the Word	57
Reuse/Giants	58

Green Forest Violin	59
Surface Sensitivity and the Density of Flesh	60
A Botanic Rhetoric	61
That Starfish Isn't Dead	62
Verneinung	63
Mushroom Fins	64
Owl and Tuning Fork	65
In Praise of Paper Cultures	66
Ventriloquy	67
The Evolution of Speech	68
Faltering Day	69
Gathering Photons in May	70
Middle Age Medicine	71
The Art of Listening	72
Snow Flurry	73
Lord Krishna Viewed as WMD	74
The Meaning of Birdsong	75
A Philosophy of Light	76
Splurges of Spring	77
Shipwreck Museum, Franskraal	78
Tender Furry Growths	79
A Feminine Civilization	80
Gardens on the Moon	81
Cold War Poetry	82
Drives	83
Red River Valley	84
Smelling the Water of Leith	85
Boning the Sentence	86
Invective Against Fat	87
Do Me	88

Spume Sprays	89
The Food/Thought Cycle	90
Prophet on Home Turf	91
Functional Language	92
Spark Plug	93
A Grammar of the Pause	94
Starched Gull Flight	95
Feeding the Lexicon	96
Travels	97
Wild Theology	98
Fair Weed Time	99
Exercises for Magic Wand	100
Body Politic	101
Full Figgate Burn	102
Gardens of Hermetic Delight	103
Background Energy	104
Spoken Geology	105
Sharp and Hazy Vision	106
If Those Were Fruit	107
After the Downpour	108
A Joycean Lane	109
Classical Afternoon	110
Interplay	111
The Fluid Mosaic System in Membranes	112
Gaolbird	113
Pigeon Temples	114
Gasping for Air and Light	115
That Sometime Did Me Seek	116
The Photographic Record	117
Withstanding Sunlight	118

Little Trotty	119
Encrusted Yellows	120
Humanism and After	121
Weather Treasures	122
Dull Blushes	123
Covered With Put-Downs	124
Dopages of Autumn	125
Images of Snow Fall	126
Unfinished Features	127
Feral Hygiene	128
A Philosophical Garden	129
Dogmas of Red and Black	130
Aye-Aye	131
Notes for a Dutiful Daughter	132
Missing Overtones	133
Colony	134
Paradise Regain'd in the Beineke Library	135
Hills with Bone-White Snow	136
Anti-Heaven	137
Shelf Polisher	138
Strategies for Touching	139
Settler Cottages, Grahamstown	140
A Linguistic Pentecost	141
Doing Things with Words	142
Hillwalk Over Snow	143
Records of Sentient Distress	144
The Composition of Drinking Water	145
On the Formation of Sanskrit	146
Verbal Flowering	147
The Caress	148

Herbal & Verbal	149
The Disease Spreads	150
After Resuscitation	151
Stopping at the Rubicon	152
Leaf Tissues	153
Spring Jinks	154
A Cold Crunchy Spring	155
Unidentified White Floral Bells	156
Squeezed Eyeballs	157
Flowery Pendants	158
Coping Strategies after Life Has Destroyed Parts of Your Humanity	159
Acts of the Apostles	160
Shopping – A Pastoral	161
Catching Barbel in Lobatse Dam	162
Weather for Thought	163
Shrinking Violets	164
Space Rescue of Planets	165
An Era of Recovery	166
This Now Is Then	167
The Body Muses	168
Prurience	169
Catching Wildlife	170
The Foundation of Beauty in a Non-Created Universe	171
Catching the Flux	172
Glorious Fetor	173
Encroachments of Funeral Gold	174
Doing Words	175
Black and Full of Language	176
A Botched Job	177

Tree Lamp	178
Timber Voices	179
Reading Room	180
Late Adornments	181
Unhumaning	182
Tree Dynamics	183
Storm Yearning	184
Scars Lined by White	185
Brain to Brain	186
How Many Objects	187
Where Springs Not Fail	188
Studies in Khoisan Verbs	189
Tumorous Nests	190
A Tropical Morality Play	191
Gentling a Wild Forest	192
Sources of Our Inspirations	193
Proud Weeds	194
Cloud Formations	195
A Celebration of Thingness	196
The Sun Always Rises	197
Helped from Their Landing Craft	198
Pace Maker	199
Manipulating Eden	200
Afterword: Writing and Publishing *Collected Sonnets*	201
Alphabetical Index	203

ACCORDING TO PLATO

Using whatever's to hand
– a pair of pliers in a drawer –
what acts of fixing or fudging
are suggested, even compelled.
As the partial, broken insect
still continues on its mission:
circling a torn wing, toppling,
acting through the damage
as though it weren't there,
as if the bee brain or ant soul
could see only completion.
Wring capacity from every limb,
send work into every muscle,
reach for all the instruments.

ELEGY ON THE DECOMMISSIONING OF THE DOUNREAY FAST BREEDER REACTOR

As large as the Globe Theatre, that language-
reactor whose nuclear fusion was Shakespeare;
steel ball of science, round as a telescope housing
but no star-gazer, rather an inward meditation
on the atomic nucleus, matter's radioactive navel –
sucking energy from pin-pricks of universe
via bookloads of the best mathematics on the planet,
huddled around hot, sick cylinders of feverish material
the contagious disease of physics, self-contained plague
of modern knowledge, within the isolation chamber
of the reactor, where the atomic virus is nurtured
and encouraged to white-hot virulence in its ward.
The walls are quake-proof, quarantined with lead,
lined with the prayers and theology of its engineers.

PAEAN TO HUMAN FLESH

Dirty humanity in bum-soiled underpants
is the main impurity on the scene – amongst all
those innocent books slackening in their glues
the corrupted animal wanders, pricked to
restless movement by his lusts and griefs;
particularities of skin-shedding and hair-loss
shroud imperceptibly the whole world-mass.
How many Holy Bibles are needed to cleanse
that soiled and suffering mind, dripping its
blood, semen, mucus, tears, sweat and sin?
A strenuous course of harsh Fundamentalism,
a regimen of unmitigated Messiah, is called for.
Guilty ever since the first orders were barked –
brush your teeth, wash behind your ears, floss!

THE DOGS OF LOVE

Their jaws ease. You had set your own dogs
upon yourself, and wondered at the pain,
forgetting that the future has no nervous tissue,
its events composed of barking, not of biting;
and since experience likes to beget its woes
endlessly into the future, you had thought
this crimson would be the colour of all time.
Time doesn't heal, despite what people say,
but something else that needs time does;
and so, eventually, love eases off, lets go of you;
you find yourself living humdrum days again,
ones no longer cursed by Humean causality
where time turns back, trees have breakdowns
and a rooster's crow can make the kettle weep.

PHILOSOPHY AT WAR

The world's tempest has stilled
to a tranquillity so pacific
even the watercolour tints
of the sky don't get mixed
up or run into each other
but hover in their separations
for whole mornings at a stretch.
This drives our thoughts crazy.
Our brains buzz phenomenology,
religions are recalled from
their stagnant vaults; minds are
doing the numbers obsessively,
with all their lights switched on,
trying to make it all add up to US.

PSYCHOLOGY UNDER THE COVERS

Injecting of a coloured dye into the soul
the better to observe its freaks and faults
like the half-translucent body of a jellyfish –
that is a heuristic definition of psychology:
inventing a proxy substance for its white
immateriality, so it may be touched and seen
and brought within the circle of experimental
method: the discipline of the prod and the poke.
Hold it up against the lightbox: see its shadows,
the symptomatic smudges on the photo-plate,
the trail left by disease, by illness dragging
a slug-like passage through the body, slow
contractions of black muscle. Now the soul
becomes a visible mystery, mistakes in water.

VIEWED FROM BELOW

The universe falls away sickeningly
into a limitless, colourful nothing
as worlds implode behind a face;
the head collapses like a sinkhole,
blossoms inwards into the earth,
a buried garden with daisy yellows
and tulip reds blooming brightly
underground – floral bulbs of light,
inverted vegetations of the mind
amongst which the solitary gardener
strolls like an Australian poet
walking upside-down on the curve
of his hairy, root-pierced dome –
peculiar, tragic, puzzled and alone.

INCLINATIONS OF NATURE

Two beautiful creatures batter each other
to a standstill – the wolf, adorned with
its social brain and a thousand skills,
falls to the ramming numbskull of the bison;
the buffalo, all primitiveness and bone,
a simple rug, falls to the bite of the wolf;
it's like the *Mona Lisa* tearing canvas
chunks out of *Les Desmoiselles d'Avignon*,
like *Matthew Passion* savaging *The Rite of Spring*,
it's the Boston Symphony Orchestra bashing
seven bells out of St Martin in the Fields,
it's like *The Burghers of Calais* landing bronze
blows on Henry Moore's *Reclining Nude*.
Beautiful things – do stop your fighting!

THE HARDNESS OF PSYCHOLOGICAL MATERIALS

Structures more tenacious than steel
are the nebulous constellation deposited
by dried-up love – rigid figures of dust;
the head is choked with a bushful of it,
iron landing-branches like wiry brushes;
crows flying in traverse the crossed sticks
like contortionist gorillas in undergrowth;
star travellers plot voyages of avoidance
on their charts creased by itineraries;
tears will not rust or dissolve them,
these ferrous entanglements – they have
a resistant chemistry unsoftened by pity;
the body does not break down their fibres;
a contamination stains entire generations.

NEW LIGHT IN OLD MORNINGS

Everything waits in the mulch of darkness;
lightness augments, enters like a tidal wash
pushing against trees, cleaning, unclogging
and wiping them to their defining shapes;
in rinse after rinse the agronomic orders
stand more distinctly in their families;
clarification forges on beyond the types
to the eccentric individual, its bent characters,
the diseases of its wood, the twisting winters.
Rough exteriors grip and bind the light
into bark and rind, releasing new pallors,
then shed illuminations back through all
the dawns of my life, a string of decades
and continents beaded with bright sunrises.

DELTAS

The skies are crazed by veiny trees
like river systems arrested in mud
or the dead flow-courses on planets
delicate as fern patterns where water
left silky traces of avalanche retreat:
all the systems hit bed-rock bottom,
all jammed together in the fluted neck
to stasis, locked up as sand formations
like monochrome fossil water lilies,
their petal skirts and tapering waists
lying in the imprints of their withdrawal
like drowned dresses, flattened, spread,
bogged down in the alluvial run-offs –
flows of creased silk, riverine drainage.

BORDERLIGHTS

Half the world stays behind in night
still clogged with the oneiric detritus
of that realm: half-thawed-out dreams,
rags and patches of nocturnal stuff –
blackness hugged around the shoulders,
infusions of obscurity into the limbs,
the black soaking that stains muscle
brick and fibre like sponges of ink;
advancing sunlight mops up, soaks
the darkness; reasonable illumination
starts to predominate (call it the day);
pools of night dry up to day-shadows
except where unconverted night holds itself
aloof in deep crooks, gashes of retirement.

THE LAWS OF THE OTHER

They are labyrinthine and byzantine –
her legal systems, her legislatures;
they have codicils and sub-paragraphs
you couldn't dream of; they wander
off into supplementary volumes, where
marginal notes are tightly scrunched up
in India ink; our thought wanders in
and never comes out again, diffused
and drained away into infinite clauses,
capillaries, appendices and tentacles;
she is the Amazon of her jurisprudence;
its natives are reed-skirted, blue Indians,
bone-pierced operators of blow-pipes,
descendants of the speakers of Nahuatl.

A PUNISHMENT STICK

Someone infected with too many politics
(so much the ears are doorways of disease)
having reduced some families to a bubbly tar
inherits the Punishment Stick, of fable, just
a metre of heavy wood with malign intelligence;
it breaks the bones and lets them heal
then breaks them all again; it whacks
the pinkied teacup from newly fractured fingers,
sprinkling tinkling china in all directions;
it parts flesh from bone like that water-
parting rod Moses had for splitting rocks;
this one splits a skull; splits a lip, splits all
the infinitives in an unfinished sentence;
it beats and beats and beats and blows.

BOARDED UP FOR THE SEASON

Bare arrows bristle from the quiver
of their single trunks; a bacterial green
makes supplementary shadow as sunlight
weakly coaxes metropolitan vegetations
from their coma, cold and darkness;
cyclists flicker through the vertical planks,
brown panels boarding up the season;
nature has slumped, chin on chest;
nothing in the wooden limbs has intent;
the densities sleep, ticking their atoms;
dreamless wood floats on stresses,
balanced concordances of weight hang;
nothing to show that emptiness will wake
to such determination and striving green.

SMITTEN OAK

Overnight's hurricane spilled the guts
of the tree – the oak was split along its
length then folded halfway up at a flat,
mashed angle. The opened-up trunk
shows fibre, sinew, the very meat
of its matter – those insides hidden for
decades in thick Corinthian columns.
Its black box interior might have been
a brass mechanism of cogs and springs,
some commerce of Pharaonic mystery;
but instead of rites and ceremonies,
of chiming and whirring ventilations,
we see in strings of ripped plant-muscle
the ordinary shame of its common life.

UNSPEAKABLE

The gelatinous animal, banged up
in custom, quivers with muscle-
tremors and thought. Ideas filtering
through nerve-sponge to the sensory
tympanum flex and flick its tautness.
Sweet matter, almond-yellow, yields
its contours to passion and convention.
Frustrations build storm-ounces in air;
appetites thin to bitter renouncing.
This is approaching the unspeakable.
We cannot say what we mean – orthodoxies
of the day wrestle me to clenched words
but sometimes blue seas crested with cream
ride their weathers across a human Elysium.

AN ATTEMPT AT DIAGNOSIS

Deception is your hiding-place; you have
a vocation and a passion for climaxing
all of your notions to fruitful illness;
every need is the sovereign of your flesh,
her beautiful poundages and failings;
some Freudian counter-weight (a device
fashioned by the shifty brain, a crystal
goblet in the cerebellum, mere ghostliness
but undeniably proficient at haunting)
has grown to nothing but a minor cloud
in your hemisphere – the beginning stub
of a real organ; that is why those thoughts
are on the loose, sacking you again and again
at will, running amok over your piazzas.

THINKING BACK TO THEN

The female voice questioning, proposing,
finally lamenting; my ears wadded with
fantasy, mythological union with another;
unimpressed by household friendship,
impervious to her necessary imperfections;
there were surrogates of hand-holding:
these were our mantlepiece gods, penates
like soft toys, favourite Escher paradoxes;
when she invoked them as bond-examples
my gritted teeth kept them lifted free of
the infiltrating flow-ways of the heart.
I unlaced her hooked fingers one by one,
ending with one pinkie clinging like a curl;
it came away and joined her hand forever.

TRANSACTION

Bluebells and crags stain the vocabulary,
taking in their current-purl of blue dye,
seepage of significance and experience into
the absorptive language, a sponge of seeing,
into the colourless, unstructured fluid,
the tractions and the gleams, the heavens
make their way, a vivid passage, dividing
and demarcating, erecting rainbows
and all the furious science of eurekas
and speculation into the billowing lexicon;
there is time for the smallest glimmer to catch
its echo into an acoustic, ear-shaped horn,
a phonetic comma, small noise trapped in
a smidgeon of language, colour in sound.

EMPATHISING WITH A CIRCULAR SAW

Something is working its heart out
against masonry; its cry though metallic
is wavering, as fluctuations in density
modify its load; it is harsh and granular
but doesn't seem to be suffering much;
it's too rudimentary to excite parliamentary
cat-calls or the keenings of philosophy;
but it isn't exactly enjoying life either;
materials shriek under its dogged grinding,
high temperatures inch along its alloys,
oily hormonal stuff leaks from its glands –
but there just isn't quite enough to earn
our sympathy – it falls too short of animal;
sadly, we draw back from the brink of pity.

STRINGED WOODNOTES

Music sounds corkier, more wooden
on these old instruments – you can
almost name the trees they came from,
wood scented by the gum their boughs
excreted, spring blossoms and fragrant
diseases that scored the spongy bark.
Seasoned like fish in smoke-houses
the stretched, strung and redolent wood
makes a curious object, a knick-knack
but with sublime purposes: invented
for the realisation of Bach's mind;
where would his music have gone to
except such glued and polished boxes
humming resonant fandangos & fugues.

THE SUN KING'S ECLIPSE

Le Roi is finding it mighty hard to pass
his painful ironies; it was all that rich
nosh — birdies no bigger than mouthfuls
roasted tenderer than marshmallows.
All this honest grub, having played
it's decent part in the king's pleasure
and replenishment, is now brought to
a standstill by the glowing red fistula
blocking his highness's back passage.
It's like a frog stuck in a drainpipe.
The surgeon has assembled his black
instruments; he shields his eyes
as if from the sunshine that normally
streams from that vent in *le Roi-Soleil*.

TURNING THE BABY AROUND

Gas raises feeble objections to the pain.
Ceremonies of breathing and pushing
seem all that's required to expel
the bald animal that has never uttered
a word, or taken a single breath of air,
whose sex is a matter of some uncertainty.
It has lived in water, eavesdropping on us
through layers of abdomen; its wired heart
has been set ticking, counting down the days.
Like a little conundrum of wood or wire,
like a key turning slowly in a lock,
it rotates into the delivery position to exit
from its tortured, intelligent universe.
It is a puzzle that will have to solve itself.

MAINTENANCE STOPOVER

Am I still working properly? It's years
since I lay myself down for a good trial
of my propensities and powers; like
a pilot in the bulbous tip of a jumbo jet –
he concentrates on clouds and geese
while all the rest is going on blithely
behind him: wing flaps, ailerons,
engine suck, control of cabin pressure
and lunch trolleys, all being taken care of.
I don't know if my fuel-feeds can still
be relied on; and also I must remember
that I'm not actually an aeroplane;
life can get so hijacked by metaphors;
it's ages since I was truly, madly literal.

HOUSE ANTHROPOLOGY

Our little glows of understanding barely
raise a blush in the anthropology of next door.
My own bidie-in trails the Mayan mysteries
of her behaviour through our flat, leaves
her enigmas like scent-marking on cushions;
no manual of correspondences exists to map
her expressions (deliberately left expressionless)
onto the graphemes of my internal Egypt-script;
she grows more nakedly anthropological
by the hour, her skin gleaming like the Amazon,
her weapons arranged, her spirits distracted,
her grammar full of strange moods and voices,
her speech stressless, pitchless. Not only her –
I'm just as baffled by the me of yesterday.

CAMPUS MUSE

She hung out in weeds that reeked of the age
and enrolled herself in mysterious sciences,
(the age demanded that she smoke a pipe –
it was the Age of Aquarius), i.e. her hippy
toilette was all incense and African love beads;
furthermore she was a honey blond perfect
for adult-rated movies of the silver screen;
she went barefoot and washed to interesting
odours – just, and no more; her natural body
nursed bacteria fragrant as yogurt and jasmine;
her face was as soft as the orchids it had eaten;
her muscles were grown by the eastern Cape;
a pearl worn at her ear would have made it
an oyster; or maybe something even moister.

RESTRICTED ACCESS

Restricted by tacit laws to the intimacies
of her feet, I glide the soft calipers of
my hand along their cushions and arches –
her body's mules, dumb beasts of burden.
I locate and squeeze the opposing knobs
of her ankle-bones, appreciating their mis-
alignment, then glide down sculpted tendons,
keeping a matching pressure on the instep.
Above the ankles occurs a zone of sensitive
prickles diplomacy agrees I should not enter.
Over the rest I am free to clamber my finger-
limbs like a pale, thalidomide spider
which has mesmerised her to willingness
by the sheer charisma of its deformities.

STRING THEORY IN THE POETRY OF DONNE

I imagine Donne drawing on the conceptual
chicanery of modern physics, since, patently,
quantum dynamics was just as true in his day
as it might be in ours, and the black hole tolling
its bell inside today's galaxy was once tugging at
his sermons and the hinges of the holy sonnets.
His native universe (predicated on pendulums,
lead balls and optical novelties from Holland)
was verse decoration only – just about as worthless
as crucifixes, capricorns, four-cornered earths;
but it fitted his mind like a bespoke suit. While
Planck's constants shot their fires over St Paul's
he spoke the grammar of pre-Industrial England,
with Newtonian accents chided the busie Sunne.

CROC ENGINEERING IN THE OKAVANGO

The crocodiles fly underwater like dragons,
their tails' whiplash slowed down as if caught
in magnetic fields, hundreds of static grapples.
Everything is sluggish in water, except terror
and hunger – nimble mental events whistle
along nerve conduits while water retards
the body's reactions, deferring them; thought
pauses, allowing the actions bunched up behind
to arrive and pile into each other in the buffer
of muscles, thick cold fat, gloved feet, gums –
the irreparable damage is done in seconds.
Once over, rhythms fall, the gastric clocks
measure out their cc's of digestive drops.
The slow beat of reptilian epochs resumes.

SMOKE AND HONEY

Bees have lined the hollow camphor tree with
wax, eggs, pupae, cells – a whole civilization
packed into one tight metropolis – noisy with
the drone of carbon engines, their futuristic
motorised flight. This fierce winged matriarchy
(engineered in service to a biology of flowers)
is raided by forest families scooping handfuls
of broken bee, chaff, stings, hexagons and bullion
into their mouths, eyes stinging with smoke;
the honey of old relationships has such a cost –
we hang off our bones, fart more, start weighing
up the pulmonary consequences of our orgasms –
all the ungracious depredations of age – but still
we reach, eyes watering, into the golden bole.

ENGLISH IN THE CRETACEOUS

Language is older than the voiceless dinosaurs
and arose before there were people to speak it;
it absorbed the yellow smells of volcanoes into
the ligaments in its syllables; the Big Bang
(aka the Crack of Doom) still echoes in its
further reaches, a galactic tinnitus heard in every
phrase. Traces of cosmic firsts can be found
in phonemes of the tiniest words; its morphology
mimics the early life of grasses and flowers,
their lingual segments and screw-on attachments;
etymological pods with DNA strings of silence
allowed it to hold its breath for eras in fossil turds;
forest humidities raised it to blood warmth.
Finally it was taken into the mouth and spoken.

HYDROGEN & CO.

Plasma and fusion define the notion of a star
from the angle of sentimental old science;
it has nothing to do with centaurs, twins,
fish, the Greek imagination, or platonic love;
equations are the portals connecting contrary
states – migration is along the brief, brutal, iron
parallels of the equals-sign, like that happy
exchange of fluids between mass and energy;
it used to be called "flux" by men who were thinking
even before Socrates had invented thought;
now ideas have crept out of our heads
and taken metallic shapes which we are teaching
to play by themselves and burst miniscule
grains of stars under their thick plutonium hats.

ATHEISM IN ACTION – THE FINE PRINT

Yes, it's a lot to believe on an empty stomach.
To give it all up is to give up not just your daily
acquiescence, the shepherd's crook and the bishopric
but centuries of oil paint and gold leaf tracing
misbehaviours in the God-saturated garden whose
highly-sexed, fruit-tending, naked inhabitants,
retired beneath the umbrage of meaningful trees,
lived in a fiendishly subtle cosmological trap
which overwhelmed their limited reasoning power.
Later on, punitive geographies of a stonier temperament
would whittle their wits to dialectical sharpness;
but while they lazed in paradise they were no match
for the legal feints and boobytraps of their Creator,
who knew they would eventually fail – just knew it.

IMPUDENCE OF THE HAND

There is something obsessive, disreputable,
about the hand, about its wanderlust,
its reasons for wanting to get into every
corner of a woman's body and to trample
her most cherished and guarded modesties.
Two things its addicted membranes hanker for –
the pink and powdery Turkish delight of
her skin, and that look in her eyes, a blend
of amazement and desire: the coupling of
her disbelief at the effrontery of the touch
with an acquiescence which gives immunity
to the alien organism beginning its bold
annexation not only of her breasts, and so on,
but also of the genetic powers deep within her.

LOOKING ROSIER BY THE MINUTE

Time feeds on disappointment like a mulch
that is nutritious to orchids, turning it over,
processing it through long tubes, fragmenting it
into rich particles that oxygen molecules form
chemical bonds with; it brightens the brown,
giving it new properties; returns it fresh,
smelling of something different, with vital
potentials and energies, something permissive
and crumbly through which the green spikes
of transcended seeds shoulder their way;
the unexpected event with its acids, sharp
indifference, its deviation from expectation,
breaks down into a soil in the placid past
which has no need of swords or ploughshares.

FROM THE SCHOOL OF ATHEISM

Skin being the body's no-trespassing sign
there is an owner beyond that integument,
a divinity in the woodland of our systems,
the means by which the god put us together,
the ugly back-end of the human creature,
the not-pretty ad hocs to design conundrums;
it is blasphemy to suggest even the simplest
stop and spigot might've been better contrived
by graduates from the Moscow Polytechnic,
representatives of that traditionally imperfect
spark who landed us in this theological mess
and caused all the sacrifice and pain that he
and his God have undergone: all those extra
candles, special services, midnight masses.

AN ECUMENICAL MATTER

When my eyes chanced upon your face
it was as if a fully formed religion
had been switched on inside my head,
complete with regular Sunday worship,
mass-produced Bibles, an electronic organ
and a Day of Judgement. The gospels flowed
and a Baptist began to preach to me.
It's true that analogues of the female form
surfaced briefly – brown pear, ripe cello –
over your revealed shapes – but only as
unavoidable perceptual tomfoolery
cavorting with revelation. For this was
the real thing, or maybe all I mean is that
lust has something of the sacred about it.

SPEAKING UP FOR NORTHERN LIGHT

That's what's wrong with African sunlight –
its full disclosures, holding nothing back;
it screams its evidence until we're dazzled;
it doesn't leak information, one half of
an object at a time, assembling the trees
and buildings by stages, allowing suggestion
to precede the categorical announcement.
Instead it yells until its voice wilts, spilling
fine detail and definition from its tirades;
small complications of bark and bud
are blasted with deafening descriptions.
Better to whisper the world into being,
let separate nouns find each other in the dark,
spread their alliances from limb to limb.

CANCELLING MY RELIGION

I've stopped being a believer in our experiences.
Stones on Findhorn beach were stars still warm
to the touch; you loaded their weight and balance
like cardinal points onto my opened and flattened
body, anchoring me by four corners like a map.
I don't think you had the native powers to do that.
Nothing came down from the sky in answer to
your signals, those extinguished stars that had cooled
enough to carry human as well as solar warmth,
that held, for seconds, the temperatures donated by
your body's cores; and then, without a felt transition,
I handed my own heat on to them, replacing yours,
which had crossed to me from where I lay my head
on you, listening to your billions and billions of miles.

FANFARE FOR A NEW SEASON

Released, the blinds crash to their extent,
being composed of wasp wings, the rasping
reeds of woodwinds, thorny cricket legs,
everything that will vibrate at volume
and make a ribbed noise like Biblical
bugles announcing blindingly bright wars.
Silently, without signature music, green
returns to its pastoral extremities, after
a brief period of enamel colours coating
small painted heralds under shivering trees;
therefore spring needs the acid symphonies
of accidental events, like blinds dropped
clumsily through all their clattering octaves
as barriers against the sun's yodelling yellow.

SUN BREATHING

Sun, coming and going in white triangles
laid across books and papers, flushes
weak and strong, intensities dropping and
rising like a fast turn-over of erratic tides;
there is an irregular respiration going
on, the sun is breathing its brightness
in and out across its domain and the room,
it is a fluctuating pulse, an unreliable
heartbeat of warmth across cold surfaces;
as thin as tissues the gauzes of light
arrive on our faces, blush into our cheeks;
the light shuffles its edges between blades
and cotton, sucking light back, blowing it out
back to brightness – the glissando of weather.

SURGICAL WORDS

Our lives have a balance maintained
in silence; well, not so much silence
as the absence of words – outside language;
we do not trust their phonetic detonations,
the more than acoustic damage they can do,
shaking against the membranous panels
that which has no name but which I call,
unspokenly of course, "our arrangement".
Words plug their sonic drains into the patient
and immediately her vital horizontals
are set on the move, tipping their volumes
and weights within her body, and tapping
stuff out her circuit into pools on the ground.
Let's call that "blood-letting", for good or ill.

A SIPPING ACQUAINTANCE

A glacier creeps down the page – the dark ice
of language, of literary form obeying its slow
architecture, the nosings of nursling and snail.
We are animals of surrogacy. Nature is creeping
into books by the inching processes of science
and the sheer acoustic sensitivity of words
ingesting a smooth image with, behind that,
the untidy cable-tangle of the delivery system,
all the complex grammatical wiring of reason
semantic structures need. A saturation of sharp
metallic rust-odour invades phrase and clause.
This world-containing object is our instrument
and joy, we burst open its material skins to hear
the music of events, iron chiming on the palate.

STOWAWAY

I was wrong – you've come back, and life has
given me another chance to see your knickers
drying on my radiators; it's the sheer mundanity
of it that charms me, like a swallow's muddy
nest in the eaves – making me hold my breath.
And I've always been a bit doe-eyed when
it comes to, you know, the world of women –
"cunt-struck" some have unkindly called it;
which I can't really deny: I'm still fascinated
by that discreet and powerful organ of yours;
you are the fairer and better sex, I think; I like
all the variants of your design; which is why
a pod of warmth on your panty's gusset will
soon be carrying my kiss between your legs.

THE BLAKEAN BODY SHOP

In the hangar of books a dripping life form
sips from a canteen to keep itself reading;
its wet eyes sweep text, its boggy processor
spins knowledge briefly then lets go of it;
as busy as an ocean liner its body runs
kitchens and engine rooms with near silent
motors; all of this dampness is going on
right beside the parched sheaves of folios
which have been smoked on their shelves
like dried Rhodesian tobacco leaves –
rectangles of power stamped with mystery
and joy – the steaming organism gleans,
its resident ghost kicks up its heels to dance
in the coronation clothes of dead kings.

MAORI SHELL MUSIC

An orchestra of the sea – musical notes
blown across the lips of triton shells
or through the hollow legs of hermit crabs;
muffled in a heavy blue acoustic where
dolphin clicks bisect the glassy quickness.
The instruments lifted from sea water
drip like brass tubas fished out of a canal,
their golden curves and silver reflections –
the sound is emptied, cleared, baled out,
each tone becomes dry and salvaged, shines
with uncompromised sunlight, fresh as air;
the brittle corals harmonise, wing bones
of albatross moan thin white flute sounds,
water's deafness is unmuffled into music.

KANT REACHES FOR AN ORANGE

The outer world, a series of predictions
stretching away into coldness, uses veils
of visibility to force me back onto my
humanity – an engagement of the senses,
the acrobatics of light inside my eyes –
waltzing of waves within the evolved
complexities of ear and nose chambers;
the world sounds me, blowing against
my mouth, making me speak on its behalf,
whistling words like a philosophic wind,
but no closer to the well-kept interior
of things than wind moaning in rock holes;
listen: a breeze rakes through the trees,
declaring their golden properties like fruit.

PUMPKIN MUSIC

Barrows of thick-skinned vegetables attest to
an ontological soundness – the round, ruddy
country goodness of pumpkin, squash and melon.
Their honest density heaves up bright pyramids,
grooved and dimpled, rucked and carbuncled.
As we finger the cool, gentle manner of their rinds,
uproot their humble masses or slice their
green bloodlines from tangles of mother-shoot,
modestly our bodies derive girth and weight
from their saintly and proletarian mashes –
idioms of our ordinariness and vegetarian ties.
How solid these rooty globules, slow nodules
and tumours blessèdly cultivated in the vague
sonic mist of language's mysterious aboutness.

THROUGH WORLD-TINTED SPECTACLES

Metaphysics in the mundane is my joy.
I like to see a herbal engine in the apple.
Equivalences of clockwork please me most
when realised in botanical contrivances;
transposition of materials is a delight –
seeing metals in the rind. Optic fluid
in the lemon's juice lends that stinging fruit
its citric vision clear across the valleys;
I give good brains to almost everything,
my own awareness stretches over surfaces
like a glowing skin; rough sensation travels
the full extent, feeling its own itchy shags
of bark, or shivering in the topless wind.
Objects pile into language to get warmer.

TROJAN GIFTS

Gifts of books or bonbons are sly invasions –
poems and chocs slide into body and mind,
something from me altering your deep spaces.
Strange, to make an offering go through you
from end to end via so many intestinal yards;
and words that travel their synaptic routes
like illuminated monkeys clambering around
your brain-tree; or like a Saharan caravan
going by with tents, tea, goats and sherbet
leaving themselves behind as myrrh and spices
so persistent no storm can blow them away.
But what lingers most in you is undecidable –
it might be a lemon-flavoured chocolate whorl,
a desert song, a star, a scimitar, a camel's burp.

OLD SOPRANOS SINGING BACH

How many times has the soul driven
a passage through its body, fluttering
itself through lung and muscle follicles
like dissolving licks of river on stone;
the soul discoloured by years of contact
with its flesh is stained by blood-rust
and fat-dye: patches of yellow staleness
show in the spirit-pith; how often has it
compressed the chest, squeezing air up past
the squeaking narrows of the voice-box,
until the soul has rubbed its motets into
the eroded channels of the windpipe,
a musical friction stemming from bellows
and bone flutes in the divine Bach machine.

ATHEISM IN ACTION – THE CHOIR

Beautiful church music draws its own
lovely conclusions: harmonic bridges
over the void, delicate choral spans
conjuring filigree heavens, consumptive
architecture with a bonework thinner
than osteoporosis, than leaf venation.
The bodies of saints no denser than air
repose on slightest furnishings, on spindles
of wood, frail wishbones of carpentry,
clavicles and femurs of cane recliners.
All issue without question from steep
harmonies teased out of musical treacle:
hair-fine soprano strands rising into naves
suspended miraculously beyond belief.

SONG OF SONGS

At night the jasmine opened their jars,
their scent-maws, beaks, and announced
sacred, brain-penetrating odours; they
gaped their perfume trumpets and roared;
their smell was as black as typewriter ribbon.
I've been throttled in ammonia; this was
similar, only opposite; it was you in absentia;
language flowed out of your being, it was
a river imbued with speech, and it tasted
of groves; of the Mahabharata; of Bible lands;
it was influenced by lemons and locusts;
your bookish culture questioned the night
your black hair flowed like a herd of goats.
This was long before the coming of Jesus.

LEAVES & LOCUSTS

Emergent wing-leaves like green locusts
sprout along branches – tufts and feathers
of fledgling trees, a temporary process,
metonymic and suggestive, of nature on its way
from one entrenchment to another, in sudden
bushels of change; other images will hover
across the lattice of brown, the framework
on which systems and similes will be woven,
invented by resemblances and some excess
of the goaded mind, burdened with happiness;
nothing means what it should mean, all
is a romance of the gadding intellect
building animals out of fresh leaf cover,
forcing interplay, marriages of incongruity.

OUR LIFE TOGETHER

In the home stadium we have left a smell
in the fridge and water cooling in the hot
water cylinder; various boxes and bottles
are lowering their contents like falling measures
in a barometer – it's a kitchen-wide entropy;
many roles occur to us: guide, comedienne,
psychometer, predator, technician, fellow
person, as much as we are able; my hands
console your feet, I am a gospel prophet
of a short-lived desert sect, or climb out of
the space shuttle with a bag of repair tools
and float up naïvely to your damaged loneliness;
hair clogs the bath drain and strengthens my
resolve; you hum a snatch of some religion.

A SPURNING OF THE WORD

The day would not convert – it persisted
stubbornly in matter – transformations
into weightless linguistics failed to occur;
birds flew not through vocabulary, adding
no lexis to their plumage, strapping no verbs
to their flight muscles like athlete bandages;
plants availed themselves not of innumerable
nouns giving them lift and carrying capacity
and allowing their transport in sonic vehicle;
there was singing in every quarter, the skirly
vibrations of organic instrumentations in wasp
and reed-bed, but the pull into full semantic
sonority was not there. Grasses could not be
coaxed to inhabit words like 'bract' or 'halm'.

REUSE/GIANTS

Before I know it, my word-hunt has led me
into an adjacent language; I cross its linguistic
border and find myself speaking Foreign,
with its alien phonology; I grab said word
and high-tail it back to English before
the delicate-nosed giants of that land sniff
my mispronouncings, my lean vocabulary –
I cannot grind out my consonants in their
boerewors way, my drama-school nasalisations
wouldn't fool anyone. Now this rare chunk
of phonetics sits solitary on the mother tongue,
trying to fit its other-lingual shapes into
my speech-spaces, the mouth-box and agile
vocal monkey. It sticks out like fluent Rhino.

GREEN FOREST VIOLIN

Your fingers hover to demonstrate
a fern-head scrolling inwards to infinity;
it must be a deformed violin whose
wooden hourglass figure is missing –
this green instrument with horse-head
is all neck like a swan-throated Chinese fiddle
but lacking a musical box at the bottom;
instead this sends its bowed slimness
with a hundred jutting tuning screws
into the forest earth, where no imagined
bowl of resonance is found like a buried
gourd, no hollow vessel cultivating song;
the fern is born without this voice, its body
is mute and something is infinitely missing.

SURFACE SENSITIVITY AND THE DENSITY OF FLESH

She's struggling with the wily spillage
of language – how to make shapes with
a substance that wriggles off the hands;
it slips from the vertical in every state
except frozen; otherwise it drops off
to sleep in languid lagoons, or dozes
in a puddle if that's all that there is;
it has internal coupling mechanisms
that allow a certain pernickety, gruff
engineering full of exemptions and by-laws;
sounds won't fit snugly on the symbols;
adhesion is an act of faith; often silence
drops it to a flatness so sensitive mere
thought will shudder ripples over its skin.

A BOTANIC RHETORIC

Bird-snot clogs the fine breathing
of pulmonary twiglets draining air
from April sky; seasonal asphyxiation
is coming to an end, as thin green
dioxide-filters unfold to respire;
everything is opening, as inhaling
tubes dilate, as chests expand in the
upper bodies of birch and chestnut
to receive energetic gas on their leaf-
antennae; I watch these wild cousins
of the library world (where nature's been
domesticated to the intellectualised
botany of books) getting ready
to heave the first sighs of summer.

THAT STARFISH ISN'T DEAD

The starfish has fingers missing off
its hand, whichever way you look at it:
an air of mutilation hangs over
its wounded splay: it is a sea amputee.
It has too little of body to enjoy life
to the full: it is a spectacle of loss.
Diversification hasn't taken hold of it
to a satisfying degree: it's the same from
all angles. Its pleasures must be rough
and rubbery, certainly bland and brief.
Its means of locomotion consists of
your not looking at it; otherwise it
is spreadeagled after a fall and is lying
flat on its face. It looks like a splat.

VERNEINUNG

There's a funny look in the eyes
of some creature demonstrating
its delectability between the jaws
of a somewhat ostentatiously brutal
carnivore; that funny look accuses
the world, the whole of managed
existence, where eating has been
organised in such callous ways.
Can't you come to terms with it?
Only our human sensibilities are
offended: the rest of nature goes on
being its cute or magnificent self
as it sails or scampers past the
bone-cracking maw-smearing feast.

MUSHROOM FINS

My hand only wants to borrow her
treasures for one evening at a time:
things that grow on her without
thought or cultivation – the maize
of fine hair cropped on her calves,
the droop of breasts behind her
sleep-things' lace curtain netting –
those soft twin agoraphobes.
These are her soul's plump corolla,
the spirit's slow fungus, with all
its colours, under-head gills, moist
gray flanges, the celebrations of gloom.
Finger-nerves drink from that source,
erect canopies of delight, then let go.

OWL AND TUNING FORK

Inexpressibility of bodies in materiality's
many forms, from sharp bony earholes cut
into thin white skulls, the abode of ticks,
hanging shreds of skin, muffling feathers:
sheltering antechambers in the head where
unblemished air waves enter the hush
allowing the precisely rucked and pleated
air to advance, carrying the distant world
in its screaming folds, all in total silence,
the encoded outside circumstances arrive
upon dumb mechanisms of jelly and hair –
where the quaking air, receptive as a sensitive
tooth, is taken apart into jungle shrieks,
crackles of undergrowth and ringing iron.

IN PRAISE OF PAPER CULTURES

Paper is my favourite substance – better
than glass or any of the wedding metals;
its yogurt and ivory pallors remind me of
injuries when trees are broken in storms –
the silky white grain of painless fractures;
glue and cardboard suffice for the mysterious
interiors of boxes and books, one containing
verses the other peaches in blue wrapping;
Japanese houses taking their cue from wasp
colonies are glued together as light as paper
dragons; sometimes it's best to only half-
understand the world – and slowly at that –
with paper technologies, folding carefully
along natural biases into thoughtful shapes.

VENTRILOQUY

The weary day relaxes its wires, slumping
a settled puppet onto its willow bones;
representations of the human are given
scripts, leaves of dialogue pinned onto
the wooden face; the world is the artic-
ulate one, having so much to say, eager
to tell about the latest inflections of light
shimmering over the million catch-points
on summer trees, pulling us into the
development of speech organs just to be
able to vocalise its teeming thoughts,
so that our carpentered, cabinet-maker
jaws dropped and we became eloquent
on behalf of shadows, bark, ice-pebbles.

THE EVOLUTION OF SPEECH

Those spiralling cords of water – 'vortices'
you informed me – like thick silver chains
linking backwash and undertow, holding
the water masses together like anchor
cables when forces stretch the wave;
or like those sinews under the curling
tongue when it bunches, peaks, and breaks
over language. The glassy blue cylinders
roll their clenched hollows, water swarms
upwards to the lip. A last-minute adjustment
involving gravity, wave mechanics and land
upsets the long Pacific forces into rearing
behaviour, as generations of silence find
a living person and bring her compulsively to voice.

FALTERING DAY

This monochrome day has anaemias of ash,
cement dust and cold cremation powder.
Where have all the parrot colours gone to,
the shrieking yellows and ammonia reds,
colours to attack the eyes like mustard gas?
They must be staying inside today, as under
grey storage covers – all the blood flushes,
oily streaks of chromatic excess filling
the husks of trees. Cut them open to get
iridescent migraines of pigment oozing out,
dazzling scars of radiation, tones of burning
and blinding that damage your perception.
No unbearable spectrums of shining today
from these rainbows that are caked with bark.

GATHERING PHOTONS IN MAY

Green froth and pink froth seem like
an effervescent spillage of brains from
the trees – how characteristic of nature
to place its most valuable assets in such
front-line exposure, open both to ideas
and radiations; but this is a seasonal
intellection only – for the rest of the year
the tree thinks with solid wood – about
ontology, free will and quantum uncertainty.
Summer thoughts are factories of colour,
millions of identical experiments proving
the joy of things working properly, no answers
needed, the mere spectacle is enough, of such
cerebral gush, such foaming-out of brains.

MIDDLE AGE MEDICINE

I think my balances are going, the dry
and the wet – my body has gone back to
operating with medieval notions of health:
the humours are back in control, shifting
their currents and wetlands around like
air-masses; bird populations have thinned;
the deserts have relocated their latitudes,
settling droughts down onto fertile regions.
The principles of Archimedes are failing
on a daily basis in all traditional occupations
like water portage and draining; flooding
has upset long-settled regimes where rodents
ran competent economies; the voles are sulky;
now even the ship's rats are swarming off me.

THE ART OF LISTENING

A dry chemical river may be spoken to,
its constituencies, velocities, intensities
measured by interceptions of language,
coloured phrases clipped to size and dipped
into the passing; childhoods then speak,
as the medium is roused; the current runs
silent unless touched by the reading needle –
then sounds are lifted like moisture
sooked up into lint – transparent columns
of transfer stand unsupported, humming
their granular meanings, alive with static
that can move hair and paper at one remove;
the chatty obelisk seems friendly, provides all
you need, provided you don't actually need it.

SNOW FLURRY

A swarm of killer bees like an atomised
helicopter gun-ship blows past the window;
we inside are safe from this pestilential
hive that has come loose from one of the books
of the Pentateuch; things are always brewing
in the Bible, in its eaves or gutters, populations
of penitential insects, causing some shadow
to fall over entire genealogies, rooted out for
extermination to the most distant Australian
cousins – the Word is pure Shoah at times;
but we in the house of learning are spared
as the catastrophic science fiction drifts by,
unlike that golden-toothed Hittite woman
caught out in the open with her *Big Issues*.

LORD KRISHNA VIEWED AS WMD

Strong personalities, pink and blossomy,
rejoice in the Murray thesis: everybody
knows what's going on, except those infected
with linguistic sickness, meningitis of meaning;
perceptions build up in the mute organisms,
push to their boundaries, swell against the fragile
containments of their temporary petals: the
pink and feminine retainments barely holding;
in Sunday School when the strange God was
introduced to me, with his good cop, bad cop
style of management, I began not to know;
it was as well to be as innocent as a geranium
in the presence of all that reactor theology,
exposed to those megatons of raw divinity.

THE MEANING OF BIRDSONG

The birdsong passes right through double
glazing: the most delicate curls and curlicues
of sound are carried intact in their passage,
the finest gracenotes and fronds of intonation;
even the umlauts and circumflexes of accent
are preserved, nothing lost of their bel canto.
The harmonies and hysterics are pristine, note
perfect, all the phonetics come through as clear
as the crystal pickup of gramophone needles.
Only the libretto does not carry over: this
music is being sung in the opaque tongues
of opera, meaning jams up against the barrier
of our monolingual ears, filters of semantic
resistance thicker than plateglass or prejudice.

A PHILOSOPHY OF LIGHT

As the day lightens, corpuscles become
charged with shining, the glossy piths
of cells glow from their deep internals –
a fired resurgence of radiant nuclei.
Into every corner of wood and earth
something expressive arrives, giving voice
to visible cores, increasing their bursts
of attentiveness, their thermal intensity.
Heat and consciousness converse by nature,
nothing is duped or under an illusion:
a science of sympathies goes on between
thought and things, an old and ready inter-
play; in their fibrous unfoiling plant cells
release the dazzling convection of words.

SPLURGES OF SPRING

Outbreaks of unknown energy flare
on the tips of branches; bunches of
tongue-like florets, urged by Ovidian
imperatives, erupt from waving wooden
fingers and scratch the air with flaccid
nails; nudged through bark-crust, crushed
feathers unfold, creased wings release
tissues stiffened by spokes; life-forms
intermingle in the thickening canopy,
borrowing chemistries and accessories;
leaves dress the trees with avian fire,
in brittle crimplenes and reinforced silks
of starched theatrical frocks; pentecosts
burning soft green candles set fire to elms.

SHIPWRECK MUSEUM, FRANSKRAAL

Your mind is an installation of wreckage and
scholarship on the bone-coast, where in their
awkward, stooping caves the mussel eaters
built their middens of shells and bones;
and afterwards there came, from the north,
in transgressing wagons, a new poetry,
to be tongued and memorised by earnest
men and woman sharing the coastline
with whales and bird islands and vineyards,
all collected like a single-roomed museum
on the coast, with its salvage bottles rubbed
rough by the tugging surfs. Curator of ruins,
fingering sea-remnants, I hear you questioning
the broken ship-names carved on driftwood.

TENDER FURRY GROWTHS

On the peripheries of trees bits of intermediate
growing make a transitional engineering
in soft disposable materials ready to surrender
their perfect designs. Every cluster unpacking
its stiff fans and collars is an achievement,
some ideal spigot, but already bursting beyond
the serene floral attainment of the moment.
In your fingers the fledgling sprouts lie calm
and passive, submitting to touch, but nowhere
show their wound-up urge to be something else –
a full crown of mature leaves, the pre-fruit of
blossoming, a quiver of honey-tipped shafts.
These artful inventions are lathe-turned, exact
components – on the brink of obsolescence.

THE FEMININE CIVILIZATION

She brings her thrilling yeast and her skull
loaded like a pack animal with the tents, books,
clay tandoors and brass incense burners
that compose her entire abbreviated culture.
Her ethnic cultural fragrance is a compound
of invented essences, the hemp and sisal
rough-weave of blankets, the metallic acid
of strainers and cleavers; and finally her own
biogenic reactions, that odour of human
laboratory when combusting its behaviour;
but especially it is the ceremonies of candle
husbandry and prayer wheels and song bells
that she brings – substance of the tribal ways
when a cleansed and lighted life is practised.

GARDENS ON THE MOON

Hard dry water under the lunar skin is
like the blue ink of a tattoo, or lakes of
the powders you can buy in a chemist shop
and take home wrapped in brown paper.
Water is so pharmaceutical with its many
aliases, the way it crosses from one material
identity to another, how it safeguards itself,
avoiding evaporation by hunkering down
into the form of a glacial dust or brickettes
of glinting ice ore, or hiding itself away
in desiccated pools of counterfeit sand.
Moon farmers wise to these fake behaviours
will coax it from its concealments, letting
the blue run wet again, into lunar cabbages.

COLD WAR POETRY

The eye bonds electrostatically with
lupins or other such weedy plants lit
by knobbly light flowers along its height;
politics flows along the knitted nervy cords,
exudations of the central planning bureau;
damp sticky philosophy is secreted along
the wires, welling as morals and concepts,
immaterial but still stinging like acid air;
everything carries a stiff statutory sentence
or else vilification; the fat folded lip
of the flower makes a satisfying puzzle
in the mind; brains and blossoms confront
each other like competing priorities; each
asserts his need, pleads the greater poverty.

DRIVES

Outside is thickening with intensification
of leaf cover; the trees' densities increase
with throngs of shade; star- and atom-
numbers adhere to inflating leaf-galaxies;
smooth countlessness grants obscurity
to worm, beetle and bird; porous, shivering
body is added to the wood skeleton, bone
muffled by airy wadding, light green muscle;
an engine of light-experiments lifts its panels
to the rays, converting and driving out
into silent energies – furious and vibrant
liquids in the impassive core of the trunk;
the green generator pushes twists of light
down its channels into tingling root-tips.

RED RIVER VALLEY

My blood like a red serpent coils itself
around my organs and sips savoury water
from my belly. A nutrient fire fills it.
My blood like a red Amazon drains
the cardiac motor and returns to it, dark
and spent, having had commerce with
the world in the shape of ocean-going lungs
which breathed mountains, namibias, seas
and introduced them back into the blood
as particles of adventure – steep, brittle-
sided gorges plunge through rainfall areas
and forgotten forests, animals are printed
on primary source materials where colonials
transact their knowledge in old Cape English.

SMELLING THE WATER OF LEITH

I searched for words for dank, to speak
the smell of that place, old stale river
stumbling through green bacterial rocks;
unpent like a mossy tomb, somewhere
a door was ajar with the dead leaking into
the day, out of their mouldy containers.
Stones pulled the river apart, opening up
its folds and layers, revealing it through
dissection of its eggy microbial interiors
where fusty gases had lain in their casket
for miles and ages upriver until disturbed
by rocks turning the water inside out
and releasing that autopsy smell – ancient
people seeping from the river and the rocks.

BONING THE SENTENCE

A sentence may be filleted like an eel
drawn from its liquid paragraph;
the blade homes in on yielding joins,
there where the coupling of nominal
segments occurred. Where affix and
root dock, the base softens and becomes
receptive with small consonant murmurs
or a slight sideways wiggle, to allow
the inflected meeting, the phonic fusion,
a barely noticeable lingual bracketing;
glutinous anticipation wets the end
of the stem, linguistic stickiness aug-
ments, and the syntactic osculation is
complete, the firm mating in grammar.

INVECTIVE AGAINST FAT

Whereas balloons fill uniformly with gas,
expanding every inch simultaneously, people
have opulent areas right next to deprived ones —
even the grossest torsos can end in delicate
Chopin fingers, Margot Fontaine feet and bony
Wittgensteinian brows; the body's blind-spots,
keeping their itches out of reach from all but
the longest ballpoint pens, begin to spread over
more and more sectors of the inflating blimp;
the figure starts to boil over, spilling rolls
of itself out of the beaker, inertia and gravity
escalating like fishes and loaves; shape goes
out of the window, a dozen meals are caught
milling in the entrails when the body dies.

DO ME

Coax me back into the poison of sex;
open your intoxications; spread the black
desire over your skin, the irresistible
malaise, let it creep like mottles of badness
along the length of an ageing fruit;
unclasp your fornications; pull the drawers
open on all your impulses, squat reels
of white cotton skewered by incorruptible
silver needles; show the passageways, mythic
labyrinths slipping into hotter and hotter
earth, to cores of duplication, turbine-
driven spawning-chambers, past triggers
and releases of pleasure, curious nerve-traps
that wallop erotic flushes into my feet.

SPUME SPRAYS

Special creamy herbiage decks the body
of the tree: foamy clusters of blossom,
egg-bundles of tiny white flowers
with a spermy richness like nebulae;
these embed the thick green back-
ground of crowded leaf masses.
A spawned white ruff lines cuff and
collar like some seasonal tailoring
to signal that primal events are loosed:
frothy herbal energy-surges, profusions
of hymeneal vegetation, an excited
coming of age. Dense flowery heralds
in bridal crowns and veils precede
the mature green textiles of summer.

THE FOOD/THOUGHT CYCLE

Food puts back that of me which has
evaporated into language in the course
of a writing day; bouts of verbal homage
draw off my densities and moistures,
leaving me see-through and ethereal;
good replenishing fare is the answer,
chunky plebian wedges of foodstuff
taking the place of my effused matter
lost to verbalising, restoring the traditional
extended substance of the old scholasts:
corporeal masses firm with resisting
flesh, fat and gleaming muscle and good
yellow pith; this gives me back my base
humanity, the ponderous opacity of life.

PROPHET ON HOME TURF

Out among the sea-birds and muscular ocean, and metallic coastal plants and crabs dancing with the tidal rhythms, language would curdle inside the brain, coagulate like the briny brawn of a stranded jelly-fish as dictions clot into spongy brain tissue. The bronze grasses perpetuating their sea-cultures demand a voice from the stalled mind-mush, a salty brawn whose glossaries and speech discriminators have solidified, their vowels evaporated, leaving a residue of ceratoid consonants voiceless winds wheeze through. There'd be a degradation of song to the hissing of dry dune cereals.

FUNCTIONAL LANGUAGE

Speech without art or prejudice is the
idyll of the unadapted; it purges and
tones the whole articulatory apparatus
like a good blast through exhaust pipes,
from speluncular nasal auditoriums,
inviting oozy drips, to the looser moving
parts clamping and clicking like pools
of lake-reeds jiving in a jittery wind;
heaven forbid that it should ever go into
service, but remains silent and groomed
like the nuclear deterrent: as soon as
the wrong side of the brain gets into it
we're in trouble; there are those among us
who don't even like using it for gossip.

SPARK PLUG

Speech condenses into droplets, winnowing
its misty compounds from wispy dictionaries;
into the notionless blue the first whispers
smudge their slur of gray – unnoticed arrivals,
footholds already established in vacant air
before consciousness cottons on; steam particles
coalesce, dream locks into dream, a vaporous
elaboration smirrs into view; now funny forces
tug within the haze; powers propagated from
clear, weightless magnets, from abstract iron,
exert their influential fields across the structured
ghost; threads of contact thicken, brainy strands
of ganglia attach and generate; thunders crack,
lightning charges snap from the constructed night.

A GRAMMAR OF THE PAUSE

I've always been loathe to raise my voice
or make any use of my vocal cords in singing
or amiable natter. As the words rise up from
my pits, a constriction settles around my neck
and smothers the whole linguistic caboodle –
a soft-spoken, luke-warm, colourless excuse
for good old English eloquence issues forth;
it turns my voice into the sound equivalent of
a flaking Roman mural showing purple grapes
and fat naked thighs: an ear puzzle, a rich field
for phonetic restoration. My chest-box quails
when switching from respiration to conversation.
I'm a gramophone with a horror of music.
Language should be silently exercised in thought.

STARCHED GULL FLIGHT

Stiff pinions as taut as a strung kite
pulled tight over its bamboo frame
carry the buoyant gull over treetops;
inflexible as the rigging of a sailing boat
stretched to inflated curves, the firm
flight feathers of the bird carve starched
wingbeats through skies stuffed with air;
with the rigid airframe of a small plane
bucking above gentle thermals, the gull
with fixed wingspan makes calculated
inflections through bumpy gas volumes
thickened by constituent molecules;
minimal flicks of its tensed surfaces drive
strong passages over co-operating air.

FEEDING THE LEXICON

The thin words come away fat from
feeding on us, our nutritional wounds;
they seek life to inflate their dictionary
emaciation. We are strewn across each
other, in the messy aftermaths of love:
smears of brain, jawbone fragments with
stubby rows of teeth still growing from them;
we bring sentences one by one like shocked
spectators unsure of their professional
qualification: judge, doctor, police officer,
linguist; these instinctive furies pile their
carnivorous hungers into it; full of realisation,
fat with diagnosis, they drift away from us
amongst the pain and the forensic bones.

TRAVELS

She led me into mysterious webbed oceans
of myself – I had no idea such wrecking
waters existed nor that I was strewn about
them with such copious textbook abandon.
I was forced into a fierce oceanography
to map the currents, maelstroms coiling
like cicatrices deep into the marine flesh.
Poetry is the usual unmanned submersible
of choice for these wet survey missions,
but the depths broke off its spindly cups
of measurement soon after readings began.
It was months before I set foot in my old
self again: unshaven, ragged, raving like
Gulliver in the secret language of horses.

WILD THEOLOGY

The lion murdering an antelope with all
the deliberateness of its strangling bite
is where the universe of conscious life
sets out its stall, lays its cards on the table,
comes clean – this is where your airy-
fairies take a hike, your gods hiss them-
selves empty or cool their cores like a
dump of wetted coals – sentimental sanctity
hits the buffers here, mate. A lion applying
the pound for pound pressure of its clench-
power throttles the bejaysus out of religion,
makes the holy stuff squelch out of the
squashed church. Those frightened eyes should
silence your Sundays. That stopped throat.

FAIR WEED TIME

A droplet runs down the dribbling
branch like a silver zipper exposing
the nutty odour of tree cores
and the damp spices of saturated
bark; it releases the pheromones
of woodland excited by its ability
to thrive in mist and clamminess
and low temperatures; generation
rushes into narrow shivery green
openings, and broad leaf expanses
covered in tough little hairs choke
the embankments full of riotous
weed – the miserable wet niche is
banked up with fat bristling thrust.

EXERCISES FOR MAGIC WAND

The body and the world are falling short
of imagination's maps – where are those
Swiftean civilizations based on feather
currencies, ground-breaking seminars,
perfect bodies under tarpaulin, food got
without death, faultless Rhodesian weather?
All is done via the body – electric transfers
of passion and intention via fingertips,
guesses at where the skin is hungriest,
intuitions solidified in co-operative flesh;
timed precisely as a symphony orchestra
the body vibrates with song, climbs through
the brambles of barbed wire harmony up
to the stroke of the shimmering gong.

BODY POLITIC

Her body fills with mind-liquid like
a sentient bottle. Consciousness, with
the total elasticity of water, gets into
every cell, under the skin, on the brain,
into the nervy nubs of every toe.
It seeps into her breasts, which hang
by themselves from her chest, proclaim
a kind of sentimental autonomy, form
a semiotic commonwealth with teats, tits
and udders, other mammalian machinery;
the warmth of her blood blushes into
mammary sponge, into the turgid tips.
The animal sits, becalmed, while her mind
mills Marxism, Sociology, Queer Studies.

FULL FIGGATE BURN

Instantaneous pop-up vegetation throngs
the banks of the burn; pumped full of
spring forces, shot-up greenery bulges
into its tight fit; leaf membranes stuffed
with sap inflate themselves like bullfrogs.
Arms up, I wade into swollen nettle-beds.
Hallucinogenic stillness holds the leaves –
gravity has sucked all movement into the
ground. The river is running fast with its
sound switched off – a slippery elopement
silent as glycerine. Its grumbling bed-stones
are hushed by cushions of depth. A half-
submerged sprig is plucked under water
and flops back repeatedly like a facial tic.

GARDENS OF HERMETIC DELIGHT

There were alchemists everywhere. At night
their forges glittered like nativity scenes
where straw was being turned into gods.
Evening dispersals from the campus
scattered fiery globules into a dormitory
obscurity, radiant honeycombs of lava.
Their minds filtering through schooled layers
of language were studded with Dante
and Berlioz; these dispensed their goods
like soft feathers of dye smoking in water,
colouring brains with indelible stains –
sharp mineral orange, eggy bacterial blue.
They spread through the neural ganglia
like grammar, sounding godless heavens.

BACKGROUND ENERGY

What makes the world burn with its cold gush? Fumings pour from the heart of the material, a chill white surf crackles like pods of sea water bursting. The busy summer leaf hums with minor activities under its shell. Flat green nonchalance, inexpressive attitudes, palms splayed in disavowal hide the metabolic furies underneath, factories of chemistry consuming around the clock. The solid interiors unfold themselves in froth, foamings we are doing well to witness at safe linguistic distances from the world.

SPOKEN GEOLOGY

Words pick the rocks apart, indicating
epochs, cataclysms, ores, glints of iron;
theory seeps like water, penetrating and
polishing; secrets bubble to the surface
carrying bits of baby earth, vertebrae
of invertebrates, bite marks in quartz;
soft mud dwellers have ended up looking
like fossilised wind-pipes; words run their
tongues over the grooves and stipplings,
gleaning a metal taste; word machines
make remote-controlled approaches and
land on radio-poisoned volcano scraps
like immortal crane-flies; words voice the
solidest substances into intelligible air.

SHARP AND HAZY VISION

Seen through my prescription lenses
the world is all prose – fully declared,
hardly subject to doubt; but through
my unassisted eyes it becomes poetry:
those leaves tinged with carboniferous
orange soften into clusters of flowers
clowning on the treetops; that medieval
city with quaint roofs and towers
suggesting witches and alchemy reverts,
when I slip my glasses back on, to
Morningside; the whole panorama
vacillates in a haze of literature, outside
forming one polity with the countries
that books have built inside my mind.

IF THOSE WERE FRUIT

Yellowing sprays speckling the otherwise
green foliage could be mistaken for fruit:
something tropical from the Caribbean or
from Natal, as heavy as tough-skinned
members of the lizard family: chameleons
or small dense dinosaurs; for those leaves
to be fruit, this would have to be a strange
new world, with all truths of the actual one
slightly tightened or loosened, the planets
all differently tilted, ringed or mooned;
it would be an iron dawn, an immoveable
zenith of time, an unassailable maturity;
I wouldn't know yet whose hand I was
reaching out to pluck that yellow fruit.

AFTER THE DOWNPOUR

After the attack of water a cynical serenity.
The rain stormed in to install patches of
mirror, left behind to prove the absence
of further disturbance, organic glass sensitive
to the cold, as thick with nerves as a pondful
of tadpoles. Water spreads the plump eye
of its tympanum and waits. Unbroken
reflections stretch over puddles as hushed
as spills of mercury, as jittery as wind-
chimes. But the damage has been done:
drenched trousers hang dark and dripping
like a skinned pelt; the curtains of rampage
are living out a parasite existence as wet
socks, pockets full of spongy blotting paper.

A JOYCEAN LANE

A scumbles of wild grasses and weeds
borders the worn thread of the pathway;
flowering weeds mean more than we know,
carrying a secret royalty or heraldry, some
pedigree in local lore, cookery or literature,
something of scientific depth (medical boons)
or cultural status (emblem of the county);
a high wall shields a property full of trees:
a rich man's abode, full of symphonies and
servants, wood-decorated rooms stocked
with The Song of Roland and Schoenberg.
The wall is topped by moulded concrete,
the trees stand in Christianity, send their roots
far beneath the gospels into Judaic royalty,
gardens tended by kings called Saul or David.

CLASSICAL AFTERNOON

Music transects the garden, every buzzing
bar of it, passing through the horn-shaped
blossoms as deaf as hearing trumpets.
Like an educated man the music sets foot
out of the sitting room full of phonograph
daffodils and black orchestral moons
from which symphonies may be scratched
with a tonic needle like a finger explaining
the whorls of an ear; and pauses to feel
the garden. Like a painter the music touches
branches and petals to their own colours.
The flowers open their ears full of delicate
but completely insensitive coils and fuses;
music passes in silence through the bells.

INTERPLAY

Bred out of red earth, the ants, worms
and pineapple-skinned lizards flow their
hard behaviours against the deadly paradise
of the desert; animals develop like head-
aches in the heat, unstoppable properties
of the furnace, ancient brains baking ideas;
I will make your body dream of me, as
drouth dreams of dry plants growing
their soft speculative drills into ground
moistureless as bowls of ball-bearings;
reptiles spark like fireworks out of clay,
ant-fly droplets form in the atmosphere
at sunset, twinkling their technical water,
developing their semes in neural ground.

THE FLUID MOSAIC SYSTEM IN MEMBRANES

Intimate chemistry in cell dynamics peels
one structure out of another and dandles
the silky skeleton in an answerable liquid;
implications of this for social encounters are
minimal; you just have to coat your mind
with goose fat and make the cold crossing.
Words with industrial tracheae, pressure
dials and laminated casings can withstand
the inhuman depths, going into micro-
scopic expansions with an ability to breed
big vocabularies out of themselves, vocables
never registered in the soft biology of ears.
Fronds of body coral, delicate as fish brains,
leave consciousness gasping for new words.

GAOLBIRD

That gull wing-spreads to my desk's full width;
its body is all twigs and muscles and stiff
fabric fans; its sharp cartilaginous mouth
looks comical but isn't – it's as brutal as a bill-
hook – I've seen it maul pigeons in doorways
with a murderous persistence unhindered by pity;
its plumage of chartered accountant fools no-one:
it's a rough bird – harbour thug, quayside brawler.
Nesting ones have the vicious propensities of
benefit-hardened clans protecting their neds.
The voice is harsh for execrations and ululations;
screaming into flight, it chops sideways a light-
weight body-frame with not an ounce to spare
on aeronautical bones, wings rigid as boomerangs.

PIGEON TEMPLES

We are drawn back to the empty spaces
that we are no longer native to, with our
creased departure schedules and bus tickets
in our pockets. Our met glances are cool,
edged with interrogation, but not inviting.
There was a dovecot we visited once, it was
dark and babylonian, a miniature temple;
we kissed there, under the brown dome
with incisings into red clay like linear B
in the fired brick hives of the pigeons.
The kiss keeps drawing us back, a forgotten
language whose words are passed directly
from mouth to mouth, lips reading lips,
our tongues tasting clear verbs at first hand.

GASPING FOR AIR AND LIGHT

Water is rustling out from where it's
been, speaking in unhurried noises;
it's not at all anxious to leave the musty
lengths through which it's flowed;
it simply strolls out, not interrupting
the stream of its trickling conversation;
water cannot get stuck in drain pipes,
it can come unscathed through the most
convoluted plumbing – u-bends, s-bends,
even the slimiest and most constricted
syringes of tubing hold no terror for it;
water is blind and can elongate itself
into the slenderest of slippery threads.
It enters the tightness without panic.

THAT SOMETIME DID ME SEEK

You lost your taste for me. My mouth
and tongue became unpalatable to you,
my poor teeth and narrow lips no longer
delectable to you – yes, those very teeth
our mutual dentist despaired of ever
needing his amalgams. Once, the muscular
slug of your tongue, primed with salivary
mucus, was not shy of our oral embraces.
"How like you this?" you asked, and I liked it
very much. In those days my phonetic
apparatus was your tongue's gymnasium,
and your mouth nibbled my stubbly face
for pleasure. Oh why do you no longer love
my crooked teeth, my spit and my gums?

THE PHOTOGRAPHIC RECORD

Photographs like bookmarks hold a moment
open, briefly, before the past closes in again,
the way one's eyes stop seeing after they've
stared too hard; eyes have learnt to flicker,
to clear and refresh the sustained gaze, as if
each blink took off the accumulated glaze
that looking had formed over the eye-lenses;
restlessly the eyes renew, something they've
learnt during aeons of evasion and predation;
we no longer have time to learn; a lifetime's
not enough; our mistakes have only just
begun to brew corrective behaviours when
the moment gets celebrated on addicted paper
by images that will mimic light for years to come.

WITHSTANDING SUNLIGHT

Spangles of brilliant green in the dark midst
of tangled branches escalate to fully sun-
blazoned flanks facing the novel dawn;
leaves like eyelids closed against radiation
absorb the glow, suffuse a blood brightness
into every liquid nook, every watery cell
like lidless eyes awaiting whatever comes;
the world reacts, taking off like a lit fuse,
foaming to the lip of every process, to
bulges of containment. The world submits,
not passively but with furious working, to
the physics slamming into it from far dark
Einsteinian distance; the world undergoes,
wrenched into root and branch upheaval.

LITTLE TROTTY

Instead of her legs it's now her tongue
that's running – in the groove of language –
sometimes slipping out into childish
ungrammar. It is the music of English
played on her still solidifying instruments:
the crooked toffee clarinets and jelly cellos
of her immature speech, the waxen violins,
woodwinds before they turn to ebony and gold.
As the discs harden into black bone, and hold
her linguistic prowess steady, well-behaved,
a whole world has been shaping itself behind
her eyes, in a medium perennially moist,
whose soft cerebral clay will one day allow her
to scrap old worlds and deliver them as new.

ENCRUSTED YELLOWS

Looking back, your retrospective vision is
dazzled by gold diadems, chromatic gems,
jewel-days set in precious metals – leaves
buckled and coloured by autumn, like
flakes and folios of priceless metalwork;
a hand-gilding of medieval manuscripts
is present in the sky and trees; the air
is spirit-clear, sharp as alcohol, with
a blue that has gone through several
filters of refinement and purification
of palette. Stretched between anticipation
and nostalgia the rarefied fierce oxygens
of cold, shining afternoons ignite our
euphoric brains and visual sensibilities.

HUMANISM AND AFTER

Water-escapages through all the gullets
of the building sound like wind chimes
or the tinkling of an orchestra composed
of thin instruments of copper and tin;
it's almost as communicative as bird
or animal noises, a knocking on the door
of sense which might be twig puppetry
jostled by random wind. These semi-linguistic
trickles half-convince, like conversations
heard as anaesthetics wear off; meaning got
withdrawn from all the peripheries after
childhood's blaze of sense; it drained out,
leaving the pure tinkle of natural forms,
a clear white physics unfingered by humans.

WEATHER TREASURES

Cleared of atmospheric mucus the air
stings with brilliance. Eroded gold from
perished feifdoms tarnishes the dry trees.
Autumn rings with brightness, crystalline
blue like mineral bells extolling visibility.
A rusted salvage of speckled leaves decks
scrawnier branches, withered russet and
bronze. The sky is scrubbed to an acid
purity; thin breathings conduce pains
of attention. An attractive yellow disease
is creeping over the elms, sucking green
out of the emerald – mould and moss
frizzle to metal filings. The day is shut
solid in polarizations of blue and gold.

DULL BLUSHES

Overcast sky is leaving the autumn
trees unrealised, withdrawn into ash;
they're wanting the sun to blow them
into furnace fulgency – cold stars
of foliage singing their fire in splashes
of ringing red; the extinguished duennas
decline in shadow, rouge and mascara
muted by cloud; their bright diseases
must flare again, fire their adornments
to feverish coal; by thermal pathways
solar infections spread, pushing shining
into the overflow. Flush deepens flush
until lampwick leaves are torched
with filaments of cold incandescence.

COVERED WITH PUT-DOWNS

I'm playing with silky white German paper
in my workroom where machines the size
and ugliness of turkeys await basting in ink.
But really I have nothing to say about myself.
I don't want to dramatise my doings, make
them sound important or winning; I've done
with selling myself like a package holiday.
The vocal muscles are the laziest ones
in my body; how reluctantly I use them
to pump sentences up from the rib-cage.
People are such patches of nettles – how often
have I parted from them with a stinging rash
or a cramp or a muscle pulled in some
deep and awkward interior of my anatomy.

DOPAGES OF AUTUMN

Sprawling, half-transparent xray-seraphim,
the autumn trees show their lights (in
the butcher shop sense) – flat yellow
livers and lungs scattered within the chest,
their lemony-green cavities, thinned out
by the season, shine with radio-force;
filled with citrus ice-lollies glowing
from nuclear contagions, their paradise
bodies whose substance has been resolved
and simplified to primary-coloured
jellies, their physical functions minimised to
(economised to) crystallised grains,
a sugary perspiration. Bedecked with sucrose
and caramel these blissed-out orders stand.

IMAGES OF SNOW FALL

Individual blots of snow hasten to
their work of obliteration, fastening
their fingerprints of smother on bark
and brick-facing like cold pennies laid
on the eyes of the dead. Thick lazy
winks white as moths or albino bees
drift from their source, a feather-
weight monolith disintegrating
like smoke. Something relaxes out
of the sky, undoes the bales whose
flocs drop just off the vertical line
of gravity. Wallops of white lint
bandage the trunks of trees, drawn
to magnetic sleeves of woolly snow.

UNFINISHED FEATURES

Those ox-bow lips (ox-bow? isn't that
some kind of river-shape?) have been
worked on for generations, each ancestor
bequeathing one minor adjustment to
their definition, and then dying. Slowly,
like gravity edging a riverbed into broader
curves, or the creeping pencil lines of
a sketchpad, her mouth was arrived at,
only to be seen at once as a fresh point
of departure – it's obviously heading for
some state of aesthetic apotheosis, but
we can't wait, and I for one am more than
willing to plant a kiss on those fleeting,
unready, still-to-be-perfected mouth parts.

FERAL HYGIENE

Scratches – nonchalantly – her perfection.
The nails glide over her Ming skin,
ripping atoms out of the surface tissue.
Her carbon-based statuary dimples
under the scoring fingernails as wavelike
hollows ripple under her raking talons.
Evolution, having foreseen the foundation
of a garments industry, has limited itself
to light wraps of skin around her torso:
elastic as pigments of renaissance portraiture
these resisting covers survive the onslaught
of her stunted nails, tamed, like the blunted
fangs, to show-pieces. Inside is an unculled
original nature of eviscerating wolf packs.

A PHILOSOPHICAL GARDEN

Roofs peak into cloud-smeared blue –
you must be able to survive on nothing.
Trees flood willingly into your brain –
it is enough to waste away in looking.
The world has already thought itself
through to the last detail: a feather's
comb of cartilage, a galactic fire-flake.
The mortality rate for humans is 100%.
Minds have milled the world throughout
this time, taking root and branch into
the unquestioning liquids of the eye.
From here, light negotiates the arbitrary
tapestry of forest entanglements, pulls
your consciousness through like a thread.

DOGMAS OF RED AND BLACK

I would say that a solid lattice of seated
cardinals might support the weight
of an entire religion, yes, when you see
that indomitable matrix of scarlet robes:
a net of metal atoms might do as much
for engineering. All those minds braced
and propped against each other, orbited
by beautiful hats like the rings of Saturn,
could keep Catholicism or anything else
for that matter ticking over indefinitely;
think of the synagogue which booted out
Baruch: tarred and feathered him with
so many curses he became a curse-crow
cawing black, immortal, iron philosophy.

AYE-AYE

The evolution of a long finger — this
is friendly adaptation. The wood grub
stuck on the end of it might not agree.
If anything's innocuous it's a chubby
worm, whereas the lemur has mutated
into a small Nosferatu-like figure with
two gimlet-sharp teeth that are used
for ripping through tree trunks, after
said finger has tapped like a primitive
sonar device and rumbled the lair
of the grub snoozing inside among
the pulp crumbs. This isn't good news
for the worm, but it works for the lemur
whose finger just gets longer and longer.

NOTES FOR A DUTIFUL DAUGHTER

Hug your broken mother. Don't try
to fix her, just hold your youth to
her cheek so that she can sense
the cool and constant posterity of you.
Connected for a moment, she feels
a future full of roots and earthwork –
she's in touch with the stalky patch
of your eventuality, and travels beyond
herself, along your fibrous tomorrows.
Let her feel the solidness of your head,
wafts of scarf steeped in plundered
perfumes, a tickle of fallen strands.
Then let her willow bones fold back
into their rickle. Quiet. Gently broken.

MISSING OVERTONES

I'm not hearing you properly. Some
hindrance is stripping your sentences
to bare bones, so that they arrive
all calcium structure and no voice.
Their psychology isn't audible, only
their common language, which is a joke.
The telephone wires are skimming off
certain choice, astringent harmonics
which carry the river bends, birdsong
of your personality. Such thinned-out
phonetics cannot be the vehicle
of all your meanings. I might be missing
confirmatory menace or canoodling
intonation. I can't tell if you like me.

COLONY

Our religion renders the native inhabitants
immaterial. There are not names for such
in our holy books, and so neither eyes
nor paperwork permit them. There is only
a paradise of cataracts and small black frogs,
a perfect harmony between the nature given
to us and our colonial instruments – ripping
two-handed saws (down go the forests, up go
the bungalows) and muskets which have
the casting vote in all disputes. Our gospel
mops up the rest. O those green dewy dawns –
someone's mislaid sun rises on chanting surfs
and dripping undergrowth where frogs croon
and life forms stir that our religion won't allow.

PARADISE REGAIN'D IN THE BEINEKE LIBRARY

In the ecology of rare books we enter upon
a fragile field with white cotton gloves
and a conservationist's scruples, leaving
no finger grease or pencil underlinings –
it's as unmannerly to thumb incunabula
further into their final fragmentation to clouds
of cotton spores, as to break the necks
of cowering orchids underfoot. The whole
intangible rain forest of human thought
may be curated in language, as effective
as a preserving fluid or sterile vacuum jar
for prolonging cancerous fungal flowers
or the picturesque ruins of first editions.
Only paper stands between us and oblivion.

HILLS WITH BONE-WHITE SNOW

Sun-sweetened, the hills rear as bright
as a full moon. This candy-coating
has altered their substance – they are
honey-combed with pockets of air,
porous as pumice or calciferous sponge.
Then things go as dull as a boiled egg
in the blink of an electric bulb when
the sun reneges on its rays. Solidity
resumes, becomes the uniform bone-
dense potting white of a billiard ball.
Then fickle power supply retakes the hills
with reflush and, doing physics in granite,
shocks their insides back to transluscence,
almost unearths them to white moon-rock.

ANTI-HEAVEN

If I want to go deep into the acrid grain
of my anxiety I am like an ant colony
sliced by a sheet of glass for the benefit
of entymologists and documentary cameras.
I squeeze along the village veins that lead
to dead ends or nowhere, just like life.
Well, better than imaginary gardens
where the blessed are held in heavenly
prisons of inescapable happiness. Holidays
from that perfection can take them back
to heartache and sunburn for a few days.
The old fallen state is their obsession,
when it was possible to err in every attribute
of their bodies and still remain human.

SHELF POLISHER

My prejudices well up like hot stomach acid.
The disapproved human being has me secreting
scorn before I'm even aware of having such
an opinion – shuffling along the library stacks
with his deodorised feather duster in hand like
a fluffy blue sound-boom, he might as well be
a claggy-booted farmer ploughing on the bald
Welsh hills so sneered at by the Rev RS Thomas.
The Almighty undoubtedly tugged Thomas
by the dog-collar to adopt a more charitable view –
albeit grudgingly and just for the space of a poem.
I don't think I can manage even that. The polishing
boom-slider nears, doing his vital work; and then
I hear the wretched chittering of his earphones.

STRATEGIES FOR TOUCHING

Because your body bulged and flowed
my fingers followed, haunted by
the imperative of slopes and contour;
clothing presented you, pinched thick
skin folds into prominence; elsewhere
buried bone formations lifted fillets
of your figure, elevated and dropped
composite cushions; bends and swoops
of arrested momentum drew my fingers
after them like excuses for touching.
Your shapes like activated spaces
announced their analogies in compelling
figures; I could feel the persuasive
conducting and went along with it.

SETTLER COTTAGES, GRAHAMSTOWN

This tree with moist red flowers arrests me
just a moment to mark the scarlet funnel-
shaped contusions with long pollen-stippled
tongues; the pause is too brief to get to
the bottom of its interesting science, natural
history and cultural weight; furthermore it has
stood there soaked in overnight until daylight.
The eye is drawn to the papery intensity
of its leaves like bougainvillea blossoms
against the white cottage wall, wherein men
crouched over books in their frontier rooms
smelling of imported trees that over the years
have sucked Africa up through their roots
into these flowertips, and made them local.

A LINGUISTIC PENTECOST

To create a new infectious language
that will carry my mind into your body
via the ears, lobes and bloodstream,
to colonise you with my thoughts,
my ideas like transferred flames or
lamps in which consciousness withdraws
and is replaced by yours, stained-glass
windows in which one daylight dies
before another blazes in the panes –
a restless exchange, one thing having
to move out of its muscular home
into another, there to work and reside,
making itself glow with action, bright
with thematic content, intellectual joy.

DOING THINGS WITH WORDS

Words of mine go in and tie a knot
in your body, one that slowly dissolves
like surgical stitches, allowing you
to flow back to your starting behaviour.
Language works like magic, producing
changes in your body like the retractions
of an anemone, some sea-coastal rock-
animal that wilts and waxes as the form
of its movement. Your mouth lets go of
its attitudes, loosens to stillness with
muscle-softening. Soon the infusion
wears off like numbness or amnesia
and your brain expels my language,
forms your lips to new phonetic frolics.

HILLWALK OVER SNOW

White and remote as the moon,
the Pentlands gleam their snow-
glazed globes. Barren and apart,
their planetary plainness folds
geologic domes under caps and
encrustations of ice. On frozen silver
your steps ascended, on winter's
escalations, through registers of cold.
Your footsteps must have made
a music of rupture, crushing
frail craniums of surface freeze,
bone membranes that had knitted
over previous snow. Then the top,
and fields of retina-burning white.

RECORDS OF SENTIENT DISTRESS

The camera spares nothing, it has
an unsentimental soul made out of
inert materials like plastic and glass.
The world of suffering enters it
as pure light; light itself is infinitely thin,
too thin to carry anything but itself;
it has to leave the pain and pity behind
as it speeds across the universe.
It travels to us in haste from all
the grandest cosmological tragedies,
shedding galactic memory as it comes.
It enters the camera, and there plays
with its optical objects like an insect
fluttering in a small glass gymnasium.

THE COMPOSITION OF DRINKING WATER

Fancy that – water from the Brecon Beacons
sold in plastic bottles in Greggs the Baker!
Swallow it down and be part of its adventure.
One is inspired to imagine it gurgling through
wild russet heather, past slabs of heavy
slate-coloured rock, within the hearing
of interesting birds. It has picked up the solvents
of a complex soil, has percolated through
root entanglements, and licked the minerals
off lichen-coated stones. And yet, for all
its earthy pedigree, it's actually completely
tasteless and sterile, as if it had been made
by a machine that patiently and meticulously
clips hydrogen and oxygen atoms together.

ON THE FORMATION OF SANSKRIT WITHIN THE HUMAN BODY

Revelations form in the meat of the brain
like bubbles in blood – abstractions attach
to capillary linings. Thickening tissues
catch the flakes of thought coming down
like motes in a river. The crossover into
something full-bloodedly anatomical
is obligatory to foster engagement in
the gross corpus of the speech organs:
enamel teeth, the tongue slicked in
slime, hard palate roofed with ridges.
Somewhere as the notion takes shape
some receptacle is waiting to house it.
One day science will discover this subtle
valve by which spirit vibrates in space.

VERBAL FLOWERING

The sensitive verb phrase
echoes, contours, cups
some small botanic knot
in the flowering plant,
some place where leaf-fold
or sheath wrap the stalk,
where a division begins
or contusions mark a split
or bud, a green welling.
Growth is adverbial or
disjoins itself by intent
preceding the separation.
Sproutings answer the mild
semantic urging of verbs.

THE CARESS

An electrical system floods the fingers.
These buzz over animal materials
as fine as silk, soft bark, moist and
gliding parchment. The kinetic electro-
world transfers, jumps the gap into
these substances, and forms implants
of feeling inside the thighs and breasts
of the beneficiary. Tingling narratives
travel under the sparking digits, giving
off shocks as douce as warm rainwater.
Understanding remains withdrawn, held off
from pure brain, close to the superficies.
Like fireflies the sensations dart about
under the skin, towing rapt awareness.

HERBAL & VERBAL

To loop a small catch of language into
the object, to thread a phrase into the eye
or hoop of the thing – that entwinement,
that marriage of misalliances – delights;
that softening to the special detente
of plant and phrase, where grammar
and botany reach an accord, melt
the existential objections of the other,
the unyielding shells of word and cell.
Without barbs or catches, sans adhesive,
without magnetic glue, the incompatibles
find time and space for these nuptials,
this intimate embrace in which each
reveals and revels in the other's other.

THE DISEASE SPREADS

The disease spreads itself beyond
your body into NHS property –
heart monitors, intravenous lines,
incontinence pads and dressings.
It cannot be contained within your
own biology only, but must emerge.
The disease takes the form of strange
misshapen beds with curious wheels
and levers and hydraulic appendages.
It says that your mortal body is full
of failures, breakdowns and old age.
It pokes and pinches and bleeds and
dribbles and calls for ugly machinery
built of an insane hatred of the sick.

AFTER RESUSCITATION

Discharged from casualty, my heart healed
to sinus-rhythm — what joy to see again
old library tables with worn leather tops,
white ceiling mouldings trimmed in gold.
My body beats its well-being into every
bushel of fine capillaries, its terminations
in fingers and toes, dispenses awareness
as a pink blush onto every stretched sense;
thanksgiving for the trivial stimulations
that fall on stiff drum-heads and summon
the rustling music of plain consciousness.
Like a prepared piano my adequate, calm
body receives a steady corpuscular tremble
of hard surfaces tapping light into the eyes.

STOPPING AT THE RUBICON

We left each other clothed but unbuttoned
to a state of dishevelment, of tantalising
disarray. Pure white folds bulged, grizzled
chest hairs sprang up like wild grey gorse.
It was good to have those sartorial checks
to our passion – the fastened bra, waistlines
contained behind threaded belts. Fingers
explored these self-imposed boundaries,
tried the catches, teased at zip and buckle
and then left well alone, before moving on
to take liberties elsewhere, but giving notice
that next time they would brook no such
impediments, would brush aside all restraint
in excitements both deeply pure, deeply profane.

LEAF TISSUES

In the greens of many metals
the trees show forth today:
light pewter, runny mercury,
the wrinkled bronze of growth.
Old money hangs off branches:
soft currencies and coinages
like groats, thalers and talents,
traditional mintages in which old
Persian transactions were done
to sell livestock and linenwork.
The pink of fired ores lends its
hues to petals moist as human
tissue, softer than fingertips –
substances furthermost from iron.

SPRING JINKS

Victorian fairies have been pierced onto
the ends of twigs and set on fire;
they're burning like small Protestant
martyrs with highly inflammable wings.
Actually, no – it's okay – they're just leaves
drooping off their twigs like soft vaginas
hanging their long fat lower lips from
open mouths, their buds half sticking
out of hoods – for spring is besotted
with its own sexuality and promise.
New yellow growths bubble and clot
together like eggs or grapes. These fragile
mechanics capture all the joy of driving
avid futures through fugitive expedients.

A COLD CRUNCHY SPRING

A wind carrying long seams of ice
is curving around in broad barometric
sweeps along the isobars and dropping
our temperatures. Its embedded ice is
like those grommets of white cartilage
used to keep new shirt collars stiff
or give a backbone to boneless fish.
The air is chunky with these fridge
layers of pure Arctic, invisible slivers
of cuttle bone smuggled in the breeze.
Melted ice drips from our noses,
a feverish shudder gets hold of us
and shakes us compulsively
like water pipes knocking in a house.

UNIDENTIFIED WHITE FLORAL BELLS

Shoots have sprung out, bringing forth their own greeny-white nature from folds or wrappings in the parent stem. What looks assembled after the event like wire-mounted campaign rosettes developed on the inside from a hint of colour or cleavage where a fine aberration seared the coat of the stalk. The small milky flower-bells blew to their smooth bottle shapes like fleshy bubbles swelling in the most private recesses of night. Not wedding flowers of crepe and sellotape for buttonholes, but pale butter-soft foetal blooms.

SQUEEZED EYEBALLS

Jellyfish behind eyelids
waver in the pressed bulbs;
crimson smears pulsate
in their velvet medium –
the ocean of closed eyes;
streaming clots of blood
sway back and forth
leaving trails of leak
like strands of red root
in thick optic water;
streaks of cloudy marine
animal are ruby ghosts
in the undulant galactic
space of blocked vision.

FLOWERY PENDANTS

Oh the clusters, now identified
as organs of reproduction sitting
proud, even protruded, on the ends
of branches; snuggled under leaves
the golden bunches of intricate
botany hang – calm, eye-catching;
they speckle the tree with noticing,
attract associates from all over
the Darwinian world, greedy birds
with fabulous digestive tracts
who spurt the unscathed seeds
over favourable soils; meanwhile
the yellow rattles droop, depend
and dangle their moist limp virility.

COPING STRATEGIES AFTER LIFE HAS DESTROYED PARTS OF YOUR HUMANITY

Small patches of feeling will be left,
a scattered archipelago of empathy,
a patchwork of still-registering skin.
This may be enough to live and love with.
Redirect emotions to the few surfaces
that still work, the strips of sensitivity
whose resuscitation isn't a vain hope.
A reasonable facsimile of everyday life
may be achieved with these. Channel
the world onto what's left, the scraps
still firing nerves of remnant humanity.
Do all that can be done with those,
make much of the sensations they offer.
Cover the totally dead parts with lies.

ACTS OF THE APOSTLES

Your humid body after love
and sleep smells of sweat
and herbs: I love its acrid
aromas, coming from places
that have folded themselves
away, have shut their wings
and withdrawn out of sight.
They are like the flared pinions
a settling dove swallows into
her tidy endomorphic body,
or like the panels of a sacred
painting that have closed on
some miracle in the desert, some
gobsmacking Act of the Apostles.

SHOPPING – A PASTORAL

Mechanical food, fried caterpillars
and cultivation of sweet green algae
on lick-sticks – this is the impasse
fine dining may lead us to one day.
Today I patrol commercial canyons
to harvest produce for our dinner:
with cloning as model, I pick identical
copies of soups, salads and salmons;
cold-pressed olive oil from an actual
place is a marketing nod to older times
when vegetables were blotchy and fowls
beheaded; I'm not tugging long beans
from runners, I'm filling a basket with
beeping, bar-coded checkout-fodder.

CATCHING BARBEL IN LOBATSE DAM

Whiskered barbel in the opaque dam
were nothing but weeds of the fish world,
flourishing where more fastidious species
refused to grow; muddy bubbles plopping
to the surface gave notice of their brown
passage through the torpid sludge. The water
had sweated off its best, most spiritous liquids,
leaving a perfect paradise for worms, flies,
mosquito larvae. We fished there beside
the abominable pond, cork floats wedged
into its distillate . . . and awaited the frisson
of the bite. Along our gut lines travelled
tremours of their intelligence, force-fields
from the sweet wet flesh of living things.

WEATHER FOR THOUGHT

The air is damp with a heavy wicking
of moisture; it is full of silky atoms,
caressings of granular spray. The day
has lost power under a cloudy sky;
the meadows are dark, their points
of flowering have all been switched off.
But ochre and apricot appendages jut
from the outskirts of densely foliaged
trees – they are maddeningly lovely
and exact decorations, dangling like
bright feather earrings, finger blossoms.
In weather like this the mind glistens.
It never tires of responding to these
charismatic adornments of spring.

SHRINKING VIOLETS

The red sprigs are being sucked back
into the body of the tree, as a marine
animal shrinks back into its housing-
bracket, those creatures with razor shells
from which feelers and fingers wave
when the shy occupant is feeding – so
these crab-coloured bunches of tentacles,
violet and flowery, withdraw into the
fabric of the branch's linen-like bark.
A frank sucking and spewing of its sex
organs is what went on in full view
when the tree bloomed in early summer.
Now those once moist, distended sprays
are wilting back into the groin of the tree.

SPACE RESCUE OF PLANETS

Minds guessing into the starry sky
swell their large buckled volumes
with writings in intellectual Latin;
constellations are converted into
new symbolic notations derived
from curves, circles, trajectories
and wobbles in otherwise steady orbits.
All gets committed to paper,
becomes the tidal logs and time tables
consulted by rockets blasting off
to hunt for evidence of reasonably
intelligent water on variously
tinted planets. This one's fucked.
Our books must find us another.

AN ERA OF RECOVERY

Gathering crockery and silverware
onto the table and disposing it
like setting out a game of chess
you lay out the field of dinner
in front of me, your only guest.
Small blue decorated milk jugs,
forks from the Far East, bowls
fired and painted in the Sudan –
this little museum of household
items stood clay-deaf on shelves
while your marriages dissolved
in cooking-rooms around you.
Now again with blue china, ambient
silver, you prepare optimistic food.

THIS NOW IS THEN

Through mechanical noises slow intentions
unfold – caterpillar tracks grasp the earth
link by link. The universe is concentrating
fiercely on full boughsful of sunny leaves
bucking leisurely up and down in a breeze.
An indelible stamp of events sinks Chinese
characters into time, marked forever by tiny
gestures that are over even as they are penned.
This magnified moment is the present. That
extinguished moment was the present, handed on
to language now pointing backwards forever,
its references stretching and thinning to silence
when the last word of the last language on earth
puts out its tongue for a final taste of the world.

THE BODY MUSES

Phonetic vibrations withheld from the air
are the silent books that wash through us
like private linguistic seas, carrying our
leviathans and trade routes, nautili and rafts.
Scrappy circumlocutory conversations blow
upon our flushed feelings like mistrals –
part chorus, part incidental music, part
scrape of one white thorn against another.
This unexteriorised documentary voice
drones unhurriedly through our crimes,
casually letting slip old corpses, tax or
other evasions. Many broken literatures
rise to the tips of our tongues, stop just
short of flooding our skin from the inside.

PRURIENCE

Tongues of difference protrude
from the bordering sprays – orange
or yellow contrasts, as one might
have to style them, being short of
the proper botanical nomenclature;
something to do with sex, yes, but
the least carnal expression of that,
when everything is so immobile –
sensitive rattles of horticulture
hold perfectly still while acts of
fertilisation invisible to the eye occur
under our very eyes; they can hang out
their clits and cocks shamelessly
and still seem absolutely innocent.

CATCHING WILDLIFE

Tickling and winkling feelings out of each other –
little finger movements, chucks under the chin;
nothing but a snout shows at first, protruding
from the entrance of the den; then more appears
as the dilations increase, and the prodding head
becomes more prominent, more frankly blatant;
at the very end everything happens in a rush
of exposure and full emergence: the body itself
gushes forth out of hiding, no longer reticent,
dropping all pretence of decorum and good breeding;
it is all smell, rough pelt and personal behaviours;
it reeks like a ferret, its small charismatic feet
look human, with sharp, wicked, dirty nails;
its eyes flash feral rage; it twists away and is gone.

THE FOUNDATION OF BEAUTY IN A NON-CREATED UNIVERSE

I swear to be true to a sufficient world
where no god's hand is inferred from joins
of carpentry, no brush hairs have been left
smeared into oil paint, and we do not see
the yellow radioactive foot-thrusts where
she leapt from her handiwork of holy words.
A tree rears before me like a druid, his
upraised arms dripping with drapery; he is
a thermonuclear reactor of the supernatural;
he not only dreams the divine manufacturer,
he is himself radiantly charged with gusts
of sunlight bearing the sacred into his pores.
He too is empty to the last quiver of science –
look upon and exalt the sufficiency of the tree.

CATCHING THE FLUX

The landscape keeps hurrying away,
leaving only the residue of the present,
has vanished into the invisible razor slit
that time swipes into green hilly space,
the slash into which everything slips away
whether you're attending to it or not.
In practical terms this means that panels
of the hillside switch from bright to dark
in the lifetime of a cloud, and shadows
on the move are rubbing grasslands
back and forth between yellow and grey.
Caught in this flux the artist sits with
her hesitant stick of charcoal trying to stop
the terrifying lurch of the visible world.

GLORIOUS FETOR

Virile swamp-grasses jut
tightly-tufted bundles
from bubbles of ooze.
Spawn and mosses spread
skin conditions over bacteria-
rich compotes of decay.
As large as emerald rings,
fat flies in peak physical condition
plant six brilliant feet
on rank excreta, then shut
their hundred eyes and meditate
profusely; their dials of living
are set to maximum – such bliss
in things which do not feel!

ENCROACHMENTS OF FUNERAL GOLD

Death sweetens the tips of branches
as leaves die to a handsome bronze.
The tree is pulling autumn into itself,
beginning with the leaf complexes
furthest from its core. It sucks frazzling
and crispy yellows up its fingertips.
Trees lose their psychic summer coat
that registered every spook of the breeze.
They prefer to face the winter with no
defences, holding bare bodies up to ice
and gales. They take everything back
that once they gave, until there's not
a single working nerve left in their wood.
They sit out the winter like dead sticks.

DOING WORDS

Come into the sway of language
you named particles of the world
coupled by lexis and grammar –
you molecules, you clusters drawing
your beauty from syntax and syllable.
Your only visibility is linguistic
your shape and colouring are of nouns
for you are absent in fact both now
and in any subsequent deed of reading.
You are like flame-fired bells
of blown glass in the needly hedges
when their melt can't bear their own
weight and start to bend into
a musical shape, a tender horn sagging.

BLACK AND FULL OF LANGUAGE

is a vision of the early universe
full of darkness and of God – just
the voice of God cursing in a void,
trying to turn all the earth-lights on
with his voice alone, like an actor
declaiming in a darkened auditorium
before the play begins; be careful
what you say, o Lord – words have
consequences; don't wish for what
you can't handle once it happens;
the world before creation is already
conscious and listening, waiting
to turn your wishes into commands,
and those into our current mess.

A BOTCHED JOB

In the heart of my life there is a stolen
and repudiated Bible whose injustice
and intemperance I have come to loathe.
All theology has been expunged from me
but some guilt remains. They say, looking
into my throat, that flecks of tonsils
are still there – they can still flare up,
give sore throats. So my atheism must be
incomplete – are there still bits of God
left in me which can cause the suffering
of unnecessary theological scruples?
It's the same with ghosts – I scorn the idea,
just don't leave me in a strange house at night
with only the supernatural for company.

TREE LAMP

Like yellow electrodes distributed
over the dome of a brain-helmet
the autumn leaves are pulling
readings from the core of the tree
and lighting up its round exterior.
Their glows come from organic
batteries that drive dim efficient
energies through every vessel.
A slow wooden electricity
powers the gentle illuminations
of leaf bulbs – a lamp shedding
the weakest of rays, just enough
to enhance its visibility, to make
me notice it and begin to praise.

TIMBER VOICES

Strenuous pillars of sinew, dense
with fibre, twist upwards into
a high breeze-tossed canopy.
In its lower Medieval reaches
the tree speaks with dark
wooden syllables, mumbling
ancient spells and prayers
from its twisted clenchings
holding tons of creaking timber aloft.
Song is loosened in the upper
heights where the balancing occurs.
Light movement eases out from
a liberated vernacular of breeze-
babbling featherweight foliage.

READING ROOM

A blade of sunlight turns its angles
towards me, sweeping a blinding
white arc over table and books,
wanting to bulldoze me away
from my position. Meteorology
and the mechanics of the cosmos
take precedence over scholarship
and reading in the sun-showered library.
The solar systems turn like giant
screws in the engine room of a ship,
driving the whole universe forward
with slow power. They leave wakes
of time pulverised and vanished except
for a trace in the mind of the reader.

LATE ADORNMENTS

When the light with crueller angles
leans into transparent leaves, thinner
with autumn leechings, freckled
and frail with seasonal ageing,
they burn with mineral hardness
their coloured fuels, the yellow petrols
in their veins. The leaves have stopped
working their light engineering
marked by this change of coding
from industrial green to old orange.
All that's left for them is to be
beautiful, drawing their hues from
the heavenly end of the spectrum,
dressing the light in precious metals.

UNHUMANING

Decouple the human from itself –
after a small incision squeeze out
the slippery soul and discard it: it
is full of bitter threads and unsaleable.
With razor-sharp analysis blade-whip
the body into brisket, rump and saddle
(renaming is the first culinary step).
Slide your fingers along nervous
inclinations and separate the appetites
from whatever is able to satisfy them.
With a pressure from both thumbs pop
the moral being clean out of its philanthropy.
Rip the citizen from his body politic,
the consumer from his ebay transactions.

TREE DYNAMICS

Simple things like complexity
of branching in the tree, one-
by-one bifurcations of twig
after twig until a haze of
numerousness is achieved – this
delights me, basic arithmetic
with bark on it, snug junctions
of geometry and wood, a
benign carpentry teaching us
admiration and indifference –
strained consolations of Stoicism.
Backache runs up the spine
of this tree as one overbearing
branch branches forth its weight.

STORM YEARNING

The weather is cranking itself up,
sliding up Beaufort and other scales
to nines and tens of storm intensity.
I want it to unleash extreme furies,
go to the outer limits of drenching
and velocity, and break weather records.
It's a howling wet ghost hurling
itself against windowpanes, pulling
darker and darker sheets of blackness
from out of the Atlantic west
where everything has liquified
and feeds tempests in all directions.
But it passes without satisfaction, and
me left still hungering for supernatural force.

SCARS LINED BY WHITE

White scars like those lain down
by pregnancy mark the bulges
of the hill, scars of snow showing
where upheavals once pulled against
the skin of the mantle, and swollen
flanks were stretched into stripes
of valleys – pale torn depressions.
In stretch-marks a minimal snow-
fall reveals burst integuments
where the hills creased and cracked.
Bulky child-bearing collines
have suppressed their offspring
into permanent ferrous cores,
dark igneous bones of arrest.

BRAIN TO BRAIN

Your words sank probes into oceanic
green and blue. They opened like flares
to show caverns of water, auditoriums
of pushed-aside darkness in which whales
drifted like hulks, remnants of old shipwrecks,
singing the pressure of depths
on bulkheads, thole-pins, timber joists,
the squeal and lament and glissando
of materials stressed to snapping-limits.
Your words burst an underwater
amphitheatre showing marine fantasias,
but they originated in the close quarters
of your brain, a bloody, mealy density
where ideas flickered like thunderstorms.

HOW MANY OBJECTS

The axe-handle is still growing
in the tree, embedded in a branch
like an implement hidden in
a picture-puzzle – the smooth
handle waits there in the white
pith of the tree, as thick as a wrist
but dissipated upwards into a mist
of twiglets. Inside the branch
like a femur sits the ax handle,
feeling the stretch of fibres,
fluxes of moistures migrating
up and down the length of the limb,
vibrations passing right through
the shaft of the would-be axe.

WHERE SPRINGS NOT FAIL

Hard mists and cold aerial grits
are keeping springtime penned
within branches; the season's clock
has paused, holding a wintry breath.
A thousand green prickles of growth
sit within the hard rind of the bark,
inhibited by airstreams that, somewhere,
wide icy tundras have refrigerated.
Everything has been readied in this
arrested surge – soon the weather's flip
will thrill messages of optimism
along measled branches; little engines
of botany will start up again and cover
the trees in pale green butterleaves.

STUDIES IN KHOISAN VERBS

Looking is pointless because the eyes
are already over-burdened with duties.
But there are psychological organs
of perception, moral sense indicators,
patches of specialised and sensitised
consciousness growing on the skin –
these are what can catch at wafts of
the passing experience, imbibing them
before standard awareness cottons on.
These will give back cultural nuances
the eye has not the liquids, lenses nor
muscles to deal with – verb stems
of Khoisan grammar, scrubland cobras
offering us new endings for Mankind.

TUMOROUS NESTS

My eye catches on knotty hair-balls
forming twiggy nodules in the trees
here and there, and I wonder if these
are bone-patterns twisted by disease
or just the untidy housework of crows.
Tumours doodling through the body
knot and gnarl its softened bones
into bundles of cancerous bent wood.
Small electric storms in the cumulo-
nimbus of the crow's brain enable
virtuosic mid-flight crumplings
and supremely focussed landings
into a risky jumble of branches.
But oh what crappy nests they build.

A TROPICAL MORALITY PLAY

He expired beside a dendroid monocot
with frightful damage to his neck arteries.
Trunk-borne flowers dangled their grape-
shot clusters over his half-detached head;
miles away their local politics continued
to eat away at the brains of the perpetrators.
The rain-lily flowers after sudden chilling,
an exciting stimulus amidst normally
steamy humidity and tropical rankness.
Human observers sometimes draw out
their knives and other sharp utensils
to encourage flushes of leaves and the flow
of bad ideologies from human specimens
whose honey tongues are of no avail to them.

GENTLING A FOREST

The forest tenses and goes quiet
when I enter, as if holding its breath
with wariness and animal suspicion,
with a sense of pragmatic refusal.
But if I am patient it seems to relax
and accept me, to feel safe with
my intrusion, and begins to loosen
and soften, letting itself go a little.
It starts to expel vapours, to release
timbery liquids, and allow withheld
droplets to fall with audible impact
onto lower ledges of broad leaves.
I listen to its new unselfconsciousness,
to the sound of it dripping onto itself.

SOURCES OF OUR INSPIRATIONS

The brain smokes like a dung-heap,
fuming with byproducts of language.
It steams with collateral activities
of a linguistic sort, phrase structures
pouring off it like dry clouds of seed.
We pick up these philological effusions
as they lift, and call them the unconscious.
There's nothing unconscious about them at all.
They are pure chaff, stalk and husk
of languages, stubble-waste from the exhaust
of our warm and clammy piles of brains.
We seize these wisps carrying their light
freights of meaning and take them into
our mouths to enjoy their ripe spoilage.

PROUD WEEDS

Speculating early summer launches
a new range of weeds, when surplus
not quality counts – nearly transparent
stalks, as milky as fingers of asparagus,
hairy as a spider's legs, virtually bereft
of structural fibres, mere pipes of wax;
little had to go a long way to throw up
these pillars of pale green sugar water;
light comes out clean through them –
you can see specks in suspension,
floating cells, in the pale interior jelly;
they're a hasty claim to territory, nailed
into soft soil like precocious bids;
something will come of their primitive life.

CLOUD FORMATIONS

Lightning draws a scratch
across the eyes; the cells
of vision burst into light;
cones bathed in conscious
water start up out of their
shut-down state to signal
with colourful alerts
like the ping and crackle
of booted-up fluorescent tubes;
optical gills sensitized
and primed with brightness
discharge their radiance
into a nerve-thronged brain;
the image of a cloud forms.

A CELEBRATION OF THINGNESS
(atheist-orchid)

Thin archaeological layers of paradise
are woven through the everyday,
seams of sensuality formed
chiefly by vegetable qualities –
the give/sag of organic tissues,
light and monolithic densities,
the smell of their daily living,
taints of normal growth-decay.
A tacky resistance of stems
and waxy epidermal leaves prove
the voluptuous essence of bodies.
Intricate red bells stand proud
of the generating bush, nostrils
stuffed with yellow pollen-hairs.

THE SUN ALWAYS RISES

Middle-morning sunlight too weak
to do us any harm approaches softly
at much the same angle as yesterday,
give or take a small handful of degrees
that even some old Egyptian sundial
could measure with satisfying accuracy.
It is more mechanical than the simplest insect,
and at these declinations and latitudes
not much of a threat to human skin;
but even if it's preparing some terrible
surprise for us (lulled by induction as we are)
that disaster will be carried to us, unspilled,
in the delicate lattices of determinism,
in the finest crystal cups of physical laws.

HELPED FROM THEIR LANDING CRAFT

Astronauts, bodies boiled in weightlessness,
come out of the capsules like soft spaghetti
and are ladled onto waiting easy-chairs,
grinning; their re-entry module scorched
like toasted black beams in a house fire;
from a warmth as feeble as the rubbed hands
of Siberian ground-crews, temperature climbs
to white-hot heat when the screaming atoms
of heat-shield and earth's atmosphere collide;
the astronauts are pulled out thoroughly done,
turned all noodly over time by zero gravity,
then roasted in their little box of instruments
falling like an outer space oven through the air,
and spooned half-muscled onto comfy chairs.

PACE MAKER

Like a silver scorpion the implant
has made a home for itself
in the meat of the chest, and extends
the long filament of its sting into
the very heart of the heart;
in the third room on the right it reposes
its thorned end, barbed feeler,
electrified claw, and waits.
It waits for transgression, for any
sign of humanity, for the voluptuous
criminality of a beating heart.
It waits for spirit daring to aspire
to be flesh, for the sin
of material embodiment itself.

MANIPULATING EDEN

Eden, that oyster in the form of a trap,
should therefore not be sought after.
It is a place of loss, weakness of will,
disappointment, eviction and addiction.
It is a place of unrealistic stipulations
hidden under bushes like mouse traps;
not so much like Easter eggs as fox traps.
The master story-teller was going to get
the ending and beginning that he coveted,
and no amount of abstinence and law-
compliance was going to get in his way.
Causes and effects were strewn about like
perfectly sprung, needle-toothed fish-
jaws waiting for a reason to snap shut.

AFTERWORD: Writing and Publishing *Collected Sonnets*

This volume, *Gathering Photons in May*, is one of three volumes collecting the sonnets I have written since 2011, the year in which I retired from paid employment. I wrote them mostly on the third floor of the Edinburgh University Library, overlooking The Meadows and The Pentland Hills. The third floor houses a large part of the University's literature collections, and it was an immense privilege having access to this rich archive of poetry, in many languages, while I was composing my own verse. I worked there assiduously, most days of the week.

The result of this industrious application is a harvest of over 600 sonnets, as well as many hundreds of other poems not in sonnet form. Actually, the sonnets are not in sonnet form either – I simply call them that for convenience. Apart from their all being only 14 lines in length, their kinship to the sonnet form is questionable – in fact they are exercises in free verse. They might better be called sonnettos, or sonets, or sonatinos, or sonnots, or free-verse sonnets, to distinguish them from the real thing.

The thing that they are, whatever that might be, has given me the freedom to compose in a way especially concordant with my natural ways of imagining and writing – taking an idea, however slight, and chasing it rapidly through many permutations and consequences – producing a riff-like set of variations, moving with improvisatory speed through processes of accretion, magnetism, adhesion. The small compass of these poems, 14 lines long but far less weighty than a traditional sonnet, allows me to strike single tones and pursue their reverberations quickly into the light materials of the poem.

600 sonnets is a dauntingly large number of poems. No conventional publisher, driven by the need to break even by sales alone, would contemplate undertaking a project on this scale. For that reason, I have decided to take the route of self-publication, and to issue the poems in three volumes. This present volume, *Gathering Photons in May*, is the first in the series, and contains the first sonnets I wrote in the University Library. Most of them were completed by about 2015, and about 40 of them have been published.

I am bringing out these sonnets principally for my own benefit, to have them assembled conveniently in one place. I would also hope that fellow poets might find them useful as a point of reference and comparison. Nevertheless, I am hoping also that they might bring pleasure to any readers who chance upon them. For my own part, I find that when I return to reading them, in bulk, after a time of having left them unread, I am invariably surprised by their energy, invention and sheer intellectual elation; it is my hope that readers brave enough to venture on these works for the first time will experience a similar enjoyment.

Basil du Toit
Edinburgh 2023

ALPHABETICAL INDEX

TITLE	PAGE
A Botanic Rhetoric	61
A Botched Job	177
A Celebration of Thingness	196
A Cold Crunchy Spring	155
A Feminine Civilization	80
A Grammar of the Pause	94
A Joycean Lane	109
A Linguistic Pentecost	141
A Philosophical Garden	129
A Philosophy of Light	76
A Punishment Stick	14
A Sipping Acquaintance	44
A Spurning of the Word	57
A Tropical Morality Play	191
According to Plato	1
Acts of the Apostles	160
After Resuscitation	151
After the Downpour	108
An Attempt at Diagnosis	18
An Ecumenical Matter	38
An Era of Recovery	166
Anti-Heaven	137
Atheism in Action – The Choir	53
Atheism in Action – The Fine Print	34
Aye-Aye	131
Background Energy	104
Black and Full of Language	176

Boarded Up for the Season	15
Body Politic	101
Boning the Sentence	86
Borderlights	12
Brain to Brain	186
Campus Muse	27
Cancelling My Religion	40
Catching Barbel in Lobatse Dam	162
Catching the Flux	172
Catching Wildlife	170
Classical Afternoon	110
Cloud Formations	195
Cold War Poetry	82
Colony	134
Coping Strategies after Life Has Destroyed Parts of Your Humanity	159
Covered With Put-Downs	124
Croc Engineering in the Okavango	30
Deltas	11
Do Me	88
Dogmas of Red and Black	130
Doing Things with Words	142
Doing Words	175
Dopages of Autumn	125
Drives	83
Dull Blushes	123
Elegy on the Decommissioning of Dounreay	2
Empathising With a Circular Saw	21
Encroachments of Funeral Gold	174
Encrusted Yellows	120

English in the Cretaceous	32
Exercises for Magic Wand	100
Fair Weed Time	99
Faltering Day	69
Fanfare for a New Season	41
Feeding the Lexicon	96
Feral Hygiene	128
Flowery Pendants	158
From the School of Atheism	37
Full Figgate Burn	102
Functional Language	92
Gaolbird	113
Gardens of Hermetic Delight	103
Gardens on the Moon	81
Gasping for Air and Light	115
Gathering Photons in May	70
Gentling a Wild Forest	192
Glorious Fetor	173
Green Forest Violin	59
Helped from Their Landing Craft	198
Herbal & Verbal	149
Hills with Bone-White Snow	136
Hillwalk Over Snow	143
House Anthropology	26
How Many Objects	187
Humanism and After	121
Hydrogen & Co	33
If Those Were Fruit	107
Images of Snow Fall	126
Impudence of the Hand	35

In Praise of Paper Cultures	66
Inclinations of Nature	8
Interplay	111
Invective Against Fat	87
Kant Reaches for an Orange	48
Late Adornments	181
Leaf Tissues	153
Leaves & Locusts	55
Little Trotty	119
Looking Rosier by the Minute	36
Lord Krishna Viewed as WMD	74
Maintenance Stopover	25
Manipulating Eden	200
Maori Shell Music	47
Middle Age Medicine	71
Missing Overtones	133
Mushroom Fins	64
New Light in Old Mornings	10
Notes for a Dutiful Daughter	132
Old Sopranos Singing Bach	52
On the Formation of Sanskrit	146
Our Life Together	56
Owl and Tuning Fork	65
Pace Maker	199
Paean to Human Flesh	3
Paradise Regain'd in the Beineke Library	135
Philosophy at War	5
Pigeon Temples	114
Prophet on Home Turf	91
Proud Weeds	194

Prurience	169
Psychology Under the Covers	6
Pumpkin Music	49
Reading Room	180
Records of Sentient Distress	144
Red River Valley	84
Restricted Access	28
Reuse/Giants	58
Scars Lined by White	185
Settler Cottages, Grahamstown	140
Sharp and Hazy Vision	106
Shelf Polisher	138
Shipwreck Museum, Franskraal	78
Shopping – A Pastoral	161
Shrinking Violets	164
Smelling the Water of Leith	85
Smitten Oak	16
Smoke and Honey	31
Snow Flurry	73
Song of Songs	54
Sources of Our Inspirations	193
Space Rescue of Planets	165
Spark Plug	93
Speaking Up for Northern Light	39
Splurges of Spring	77
Spoken Geology	105
Spring Jinks	154
Spume Sprays	89
Squeezed Eyeballs	157
Starched Gull Flight	95

Stopping at the Rubicon	152
Storm Yearning	184
Stowaway	45
Strategies for Touching	139
String Theory in the Poetry of Donne	29
Stringed Woodnotes	22
Studies in Khoisan Verbs	189
Sun Breathing	42
Surface Sensitivity and the Density of Flesh	60
Surgical Words	43
Tender Furry Growths	79
That Sometime Did Me Seek	116
That Starfish Isn't Dead	62
The Art of Listening	72
The Blakean Body Shop	46
The Body Muses	168
The Caress	148
The Composition of Drinking Water	145
The Disease Spreads	150
The Dogs of Love	4
The Evolution of Speech	68
The Fluid Mosaic System in Membranes	112
The Food/Thought Cycle	90
The Foundation of Beauty in a Non-Created Universe	171
The Hardness of Psychological Material	9
The Laws of the Other	13
The Meaning of Birdsong	75
The Photographic Record	117
The Sun Always Rises	197
The Sun King's Eclipse	23

Thinking Back to Then	19
This Now Is Then	167
Through World-Tinted Spectacles	50
Timber Voices	179
Transaction	20
Travels	97
Tree Dynamics	183
Tree Lamp	178
Trojan Gifts	51
Tumorous Nests	190
Turning the Baby Around	24
Unfinished Features	127
Unhumaning	182
Unidentified White Floral Bells	156
Unspeakable	17
Ventriloquy	67
Verbal Flowering	147
Verneinung	63
Viewed From Below	7
Weather for Thought	163
Weather Treasures	122
Where Springs Not Fail	188
Wild Theology	98
Withstanding Sunlight	118

Milton Keynes UK
Ingram Content Group UK Ltd.
UKHW040616160823
426897UK00007B/123